FAITH GOIMARAC RALPHS

PLANT-BASED

COOKING FOR

Kids

Dedicated to my mom, who supported my interest in the kitchen as a child even though it was messy and slow, and who made family meals a priority.

A special thank-you to the following individuals (and many more!) who helped with the process of making this cookbook!

- Alicia Schick
- Tiffany Mortensen
- Tasha McClatchy
- Sarah Gardener
- Brittany Graham
- Janice Goimarac
- Carson Ralphs
- Carrie Perrine

Text copyright © 2022 by Faith Ralphs
Recipe photography by Leslie Rodriguez and Faith Ralphs

Published by Bushel & Peck Books, www.bushelandpeckbooks.com.

Bushel & Peck Books is dedicated to fighting illiteracy all over the world. For every book we sell, we donate one to a child in need—book for book. To nominate a school or organization to receive free books, please visit www.bushelandpeckbooks.com.

LCCN: 2022909226 ISBN: 9781638191322

First Edition Printed in China 10 9 8 7 6 5 4 3

Additional photography and graphics licensed from Shutterstock.com as follows: cover doodles: Kraphix, Nastya Verich, and ; cover photo of girl with vegetables: Yana; cover photo of avocado: AtlasStudio; nutritional yeast: ; mustard: Chursina Viktoriia; guacamole: ; bowl of shredded carrot: New Africa; shredded carrot on white: SeDmi; tofu block: TanyaKim; wrapped burrito: alisafarov; bowl of flax seeds: Pixel-Shot; bowl of chia seeds: Irina Shatilova; bowl of almond butter: Sheila Fitzgerald; "no" icon: Uswa KDT; corn tortilla: Ilia Nesolenyi; applesauce: Michelle Lee Photography; sunflower seed butter: BW Folsom; bowl of mashed banana: bigacis; potatoes: Perry Correll; whole grain spaghetti: Anna Hoychuk; bowl of alphabet pasta: Peter Hermes Furian; bowl of white beans: deniol09; soaking almonds: Enlightened Media; lasagna noodles: Fotos593; cream cheese: Kristi Blokhin; yogurt: Julia Sudnitskaya; cornmeal bowl: voyager_human; almond flour: Sea Wave; flour: Didecs; walnuts: Michelle Lee Photography; soy milk: Love the wind; grain macaroni: Maja Drazic; lettuce leaf: Varts; bun: theshots.co; whole grain pasta: rodrigobark; oil: Anton Starikov; banana breakfast porridge: Tatiana Volgutova; tofu bowl: sweetsake; jackfruit: moolek skee; black beans: focal point; ginger and garlic: StockImageFactory.com; cream in blender: HealthyLauraCom; hummus: BarbaraGoreckaPhotography; blue bowl: Ratana Prongjai; fruits and vegetables on white: StudioPhotoDFlorez; strawberry blueberry oatmeal: Julia Sudnitskaya; banana almond butter oatmeal: New Africa; mango bowl: TinasDreamworld; apple slices: Tobik; canisters of grain: Erhan Inga; strawberries: Daria Medvedeva; tomato, cucumber, and onion: Nataly Studio; carrots and peppers: Natasha Breen; green peas: Jiri Hera; spoon icon: Rainboska; bowl of chopped peppers: Wytsnsr; coin purse: StudioPhotoDFlorez; kale: StudioPhotoDFlorez; salad: Aleksey Bobyliov; chili pepper: Ozgur Senergin; cashew spoon: NIKCOA; cocoa powder spoon: xpixel; flax seed spoon: koosen; flour spoon: piotr szczepanek; almond flour spoon: Pixel-Shot; yeast spoon: BestPix; oil spoon: MaraZe; avocado oil: Food Impressions; milk spoon: EvgeniiAnd; salt spoon: Bphoto-art; hemp seeds spoon: MAHATHIR MOHD YASIN; pumpkin seeds spoon: pukao; chocolate chips spoon: Sutipong Arsirapoj; soy sauce spoon: Olha Kozachenko; dates spoon: ShutterOK; coconut sugar: xpixel; mashed banana spoon: bigacis; taco seasoning spoon: BW Folsom; tahini spoon: Pixel-Shot; tofu fork: Prostock-studio; watermelon cookie cutter: Flaffy; minced garlic: Ermak Oksana; sliced citrus: HannandWolf; diced onion: Alexey Kabanov; chopped pepper: bigacis; measuring spoons: Elena Elisseeva; girl slicing strawberries: ucchie79; kiwi oatmeal: 5 second Studio; pasta: mockupline.com; sliced vegetables: baibaz, Craevschii Family; pasta bowl: Nataly Studio; green peas: MasterQ; mango: StudioPhotoDFlorez; kale chips: New Africa; carrots: StudioPhotoDFlorez; strawberries: New Africa; almonds: Hong Vo; broken chocolate: Nataly Studio; sliced fruit: StudioPhotoDFlorez; honey: New Africa; granola spoon: Oksana Mizina; sweet potato fries: Camerasandcoffee; sliced peppers: PJjaruwan; Instapot icon: jekitut; cooking pot: Vectorchok; oven: Zarit; microwave: Oakview Studios; salt spoon: Alena A; soy sauce spoon: timquo; honey spoon: xpixel; peanut butter spoon: Rutina; popcorn box: Makistock; blueberries hand: Elena Fedorina; banana hand: s_oleg; carrot peeling: Yury Nikolaev; fork mashed banana: Sarah Marchant; berries background: Foxys Forest Manufacture; beets: StudioPhotoDFlorez; cocoa powder bowl: Jiri Hera; frosting bowl: casanisa; dates bowl: bigacis; beet smoothie: BBA Photography; green smoothie: Magdanatka; chocolate milkshake: Karlisz; peanut butter: New Africa; spoon wheat pasta: Maja Drazic; chickpeas: Jiri Hera; chickpeas bowl: Moving Moment; refried beans: Mironov Vladimir; sauce: Ryzhkov Photography; broccoli: MasterQ; corn tortilla: Binh Thanh Bui; energy balls: miss.lemon; lunch container: Mehmet Recep Ozdemir; grocery bag: Marharyta Kovalenko; wheat spaghetti: bigacis; cilantro: Diana Taliun; peanuts: Rattana Anukun; pumpkin seeds bowl: everydayplus; diced potato: Kaiskynet Studio; sliced carrot: Africa Studio; mashed potato: Karpenkov Denis; bowl of potatoes: Zilu8; pineapple circle: Leelakajonkij; scattered alphabet pasta: ALEX S; wheat toast: samantha grandy; almond flour: Diana Taliun; soy sauce bowl: Kritchai7752; tahini bowl: Julia Sudnitskaya; broccoli bowl: New Africa; diced tofu: bigacis; cauliflower rice: Anna Puzatykh; lentils bowl: Peter Hermes Furian; pico de gallo: Africa Studio; lentils scattered: SOMMAI; cooked lentils: Moving Moment; crumbled tofu: Peter Hermes Furian; rice: AmyLv; hominy: Michelle Lee Photography; pot with steam: AlenKadr; hummus flavors: zi3000; chocolate hummus: Daria Arnautova; coconut: kireewong foto; lemon juice: Viktorl; lettuce: grey_and; falling carrots: grey_and; squeezed lemon: Africa Studio; sliced onion: Nattika; falling strawberries: Olga Guchek; falling pecans: grey_and; energy bites: Olga Dubravina; energy bites in coconut: Mila Naumova; spinach in bowl: Sunny Forest; sliced banana: timquo; clover: Africa Studio and Lyudmila Mikhailovskaya; spice: Katarzyna Hurova; apples: Nataly Studio; celery: bigacis; frozen banana: Atsushi Hirao; dried fruits and nuts: nadianb; strawberries in bowl: yingko; pistachios: lewalp; kale chips bowl: Marharyta M; paprika: Chursina Viktoriia; ranch: Derek Brumby; sliced tomatoes and cucumbers: Jacek Fulawka; gravy: Africa Creative Family; yellow sauce: MaraZe; mustard sauce: Spalnic; maple balsamic: Karpenkov Denis; chia jam: Nelli Syrotynska; raspberries: New Africa; frozen grapes: Creative Family; mango turtle: Nataly Studio; banana toast: sedir; honey dipper: NIKCOA; frozen peas: motorolka; sliced oranges: baibaz; coconut flakes: New Africa; grapes: Evgeny Tomeev; chocolate chip cookie: Sergio33; blueberries: Anton Starikov; fruit snacks: aperturesound; black beans bowl: Natalia Wimberley; chocolate chips bowl: Michelle Lee Photography; corn bowl: New Africa; corn chips: MaraZe; raisins bowl: Natalya Yudina; sliced almonds: Peter Hermes Furian; caramel sauce: bigacis; sliced lime: mama_mia; mandarin oranges: Moving Moment; chocolate cream: Oliver Wilde; mixer with chocolate: Arina P Habich; coconut sugar bowl: Geshas; honey drips: New Africa; peaches: D_M; groceries: VasiliyBudarin; potato chips: bigacis; Hostess cupcake: kuhn50; orange slices: Nattika; celery sticks: grey_and; juice bottle: New Africa; apples: StudioPhotoDFlorez; colored candies: Evikka; cereal: Hong Vo; almonds: LAURA_VN; watermelon: Indigo Photo Club; party: Norb_KM; blue plate: Dewin ID; pink plate and napkin: Natali Samoro; striped straws: homydesign; flour canister: Afonkin_Y; measuring cup icon: Art studio G; sunflower seeds: bigacis; whole wheat flour spoon: Morinka; berry syrup: Shebeko; cover blueberries: Tanya Sid; cover strawberry: AmyLv; cover peas: Eywa; endpapers pattern: lena_nikolaeva.

FAITH GOIMARAC RALPHS

PLANT-BASED

COOKING FOR

Kids

A PLANT-BASED FAMILY COOKBOOK WITH OVER

70

whole-food,
plant-based
recipes for
kids

BUSHEL
& PECK
BOOKS

CONTENTS

INTRODUCTION

Ever since I was a kid, I loved going to the cookbook section in the children's area of the library. I loved to look through the pictures and try new recipes. As an adult who has transitioned to a whole-food, plant-based lifestyle, I now notice that kids' cookbooks are almost all filled with ingredients that have little to no micronutrients—they contain loads of refined flour, sugar, cheese, meat, and not enough fruits and vegetables (or pictures!). I knew I needed to show kids and families that easy, healthy, fun, and delicious *can* all coexist.

Some people have the attitude that it doesn't matter what kids eat, that they just need calories for now and they will grow into healthier habits to make up for the poor dietary choices of their childhood. However, our kids deserve a better, more honest attitude. The nutrition they get in those early years of life sets them up for their future health (and habits!).

The way we currently feed children in the U.S. isn't ideal. The health of our children is failing. Asthma, eczema, ear infections, anxiety, depression, and constipation have become very common among children[1], and nearly 1 out of 5 adolescents are obese or prediabetic.[2] These conditions can often be prevented and alleviated through a nourished and strong immune system and a healthy gut microbiome, all of which are more attainable on a plant-based diet.[3]

Without being taught to cook, our children are stuck with the food our society offers them and vigorously markets to them: the standard American diet. This diet has too many empty calories, not enough disease-preventing antioxidants and phytochemicals, and leads to the standard American diseases.

On the other hand, teaching your children to cook with whole plant foods can change their lives! With the environmental benefits of a plant-based diet (more on that later), not to mention the health benefits, it can even change the world. In the short term, your kids will enjoy time with you and will soak up kitchen knowledge. Over a lifetime, they will feel at peace with food, have confidence in their cooking skills, save themselves tremendous amounts of money, avoid many health complications, and have happy food-related memories. What a gift!

Consider this book a toddler-to-teenager cookbook. Your toddlers can sit by you as you make the recipes at first, then slowly start to participate more and more until, in the blink of an eye, they are leaving home (tears!) with confidence that they can feed themselves and with their favorite recipes etched into their memories after making them so many times.

While this is technically a book of recipes for kids, rest assured, I love every dish in this book as an adult! They are tried and true and are some of my family's very favorite recipes. The Lentil Tacos (see page 97) and Stir-Fry (see page 93) are probably my favorite quick dinners, and we make Chocolate Cherry Nice Cream (see page 171) as a family night treat more than anything else. And thank goodness adults enjoy these recipes, because the number-one predictor of what children eat is what they see their parents eat!

> If we eat the standard American diet, we will likely get the standard American diseases.

*Y*ou work for an hour preparing a healthy meal, you all sit down to eat—and your kids refuse to put a bite in their mouths. Suddenly you become a short-order cook, making something totally different for each kid in *addition* to the meal you just prepared. Instead of dinner being the highlight of your day, it's heck.

I've been there, and I still have days like that. However, some of it is self-imposed. It all comes down to properly understanding the shared mealtime responsibilities of parents and children. Ellyn Satter, a feeding therapist and psychotherapist, illustrates it this way:

FRAMEWORK 1: SHARED RESPONSIBILITIES

PARENT'S RESPONSIBILITY — DECIDE WHAT, WHEN, AND WHERE TO EAT · DECIDE HOW MUCH AND IF TO EAT — **CHILDREN'S RESPONSIBILITY**

FRAMEWORK 2: GUIDING RULES

I personally like to think of it as a set of habits or rules. When I am consistent with these rules, my children usually *do* eat bowls of lentil soup and steamed broccoli! Here are my guiding rules:

- Don't offer children different food because they don't like what's being served. It's hard to watch them not eat, but be strong; they are just testing the limits.

- Don't make a big deal if children won't eat. Play it cool. Ignore it. Talk about other things. Remember that pressure will only create more avoidance. Offer them a different healthy snack later on, if needed (of your choosing, not theirs).

- Have set meal and snack times and try your best to only eat at those times. Avoid snacking for 1-2 hours before a meal so that your kids will be hungry and more willing to eat what's served.

- Have something on the table you know everyone will enjoy. If you know your child will struggle to like the main dish, serve a healthy side dish you know he or she will eat (orange slices, avocado, peas, berries, rice, etc.) so that you can all eat happily together and still allow freedom of choice. This keeps things healthy while avoiding the power struggle.

Be consistent, stick to these rules, and, with time and patience, you will have children who will happily eat whatever you eat.

SOME FANTASTIC RESOURCES FOR OVERCOMING PICKY EATING:

If you'd like to learn more about helping picky eaters, here are some terrific books I recommend:

- *French Kids Eat Everything* by Karen Le Billon
- *Getting to Yum: The 7 Secrets to Raising Picky Eaters* by Karen Le Billon
- *Boundaries with Kids* by Henry Cloud and John Townsend
- *A Parent's Guide to Intuitive Eating: How to Raise Kids Who Love to Eat Healthy* by Dr. Yami Cazorla-Lancaster

WHAT IS A WHOLE-FOOD, PLANT-BASED DIET?

whole-food, plant-based way of eating is one that includes thousands of delicious plants but no processed or animal foods.

WHOLE FOODS are foods that have not had part of the food taken away. Apples, for example, come straight off a tree, and when you eat one, you are eating the whole food. Apple juice has had a lot of the apple taken away and is no longer a whole food. Peanuts are a whole food, but peanut oil is not, since most of the peanut was taken away. Peanut butter (made of just peanuts) is also considered a whole food because no part of the peanut

has been taken away; the form has just changed.

PLANT FOODS are foods that come from plants, not animals. A whole-food, plant-based diet consists of fruits, vegetables, grains, legumes (beans, lentils, and peas), nuts, and seeds.

The difference between a vegan diet and a whole-food, plant-based diet is that vegan diets include processed foods. Oreo cookies and potato chips are technically vegan, but they aren't whole foods and are not nutritious. However, all whole plant foods are a healthy, nutritious choice!

If you're changing to a whole-food, plant-based lifestyle, you might feel like there are a lot of foods you can't eat. If you feel that way, consider making a list of all the whole plant foods you like and put it on your fridge. You'll discover that there are literally thousands of options you *can* eat!

DO YOU NEED TO BE 100% WHOLE-FOOD, PLANT-BASED TO GET THE BENEFITS?

Several experts agree that at least 90% compliance is best. Although you're free to eat 100% whole plant foods, many people find that unsustainable long-term. Joel Fuhrman, a whole-food, plant-based expert and doctor, recommends that no more than 10% of our calories come from processed or animal foods each day. If you eat 1,500 calories a day, then up to 150 calories a day could come from processed or animal foods (that's about the same as the the calories in a cookie, a handful of chips or crackers, a tablespoon of oil, or a slice of cheese). This cookbook follows the 90/10 rule, in that some flour tortillas, breadcrumbs, chocolate chips, etc., are used (but not required). There are always options to exclude those processed ingredients and make it 100% unprocessed. Everyone is at a different place in their journey, and you can adjust these recipes to where you're at. This book is written with the beginner in mind, who might not be used to eating this way yet.

WHY WHOLE-FOOD, PLANT-BASED?

There are several reasons, both for you and the planet, to eat a whole-food, plant-based diet. Take a look!

FOR YOUR BODY

This way of eating . . .

- Drastically decreases chances of diabetes, cancer, and other chronic diseases.
- Decreases common childhood ailments such as constipation[4], ear infections, frequent colds[5], and asthma.[6]
- Makes it easier to maintain a healthy weight.
- Provides more nutrition, since all whole, plant foods are nutrient-dense. Nutrition = power for your body!
- Promotes healthier gut bacteria because of the quantity and diversity of fiber.

- Prevents heart disease, since plant foods never contain any cholesterol and almost never contain saturated fat.
- Is proven to help improve mental health.[7]

For further details on the why and how of a plant-based diet for children, and how to cover all nutritional requirements, I recommend the book *The Plant-Based Baby and Toddler* by Alexandra Caspero and Whitney English (both registered dieticians).

FOR YOUR WALLET

You have more exciting things you want to spend money on than food, right? Most whole plant foods are very affordable. The cheapest healthy foods are all staples of a whole-food, plant-based diet: potatoes, rice, beans, lentils, oats, fruits, and vegetables. Although nuts, seeds, and sweeteners like maple syrup or dates can get expensive, it evens out, since you won't be spending money on meat, dairy, and processed foods.

Buying from bulk sections can also help keep costs down. Buying frozen fruits and vegetables is often cheaper and is equally (or more) nutritious as fresh.

Aside from groceries, you may also eventually save thousands of dollars by avoiding medical bills and prescriptions.

FOR THE PLANET

Eating whole-food and plant-based is also the best way to eat to protect the earth and the environment! Diets rich in animal products require a lot of water, land, and grain. A 2019 *Lancet* report noted that "almost two-thirds of all soybeans, maize, barley, and about a third of all grains are used as feed for animals."[8] All that plant food would go much farther to alleviate world hunger if fed to people instead of animals raised for food.

Since producing meat requires growing a lot of feed, eating less meat saves a tremendous amount of water. It takes about 450 gallons of water to produce one quarter-pound hamburger (one meal), whereas it only takes 39 gallons to produce a pound of vegetables![9]

HOW TO START EATING WHOLE-FOOD, PLANT-BASED

How do you start to eat whole-food and plant-based? Here are three tips.

1 MODIFY THE MEALS YOU ALREADY LIKE. Instead of cow milk and cereal, choose plant milk and a whole-grain, low-sugar cereal or homemade granola or oatmeal. Instead of spaghetti with white pasta, beef, and cheese, make whole-grain spaghetti noodles with lentils or diced veggies in the sauce. Instead of ham and cheese sandwiches, make avocado and tomato sandwiches or peanut butter banana sandwiches. Instead of tacos with meat, make lentil, black bean, or tofu tacos.

2 CHANGE WHAT YOU BUY. It all starts with your grocery list! Start buying way more fruits and vegetables and plan your meals around them. Try to avoid buying overly processed foods—they can be addictive. If it's in your house, it will be in your mouth. With time, your taste buds will change, and you will truly enjoy plant foods much more than ever before. I promise!

3 **MAKE YOUR OWN CONVENIENCE FOODS**. Since you're basically only buying ingredients, you'll need to learn to turn those ingredients into quick and easy food. Make breakfast cookies, muffins, burritos, veggie burger patties, or taquitos and freeze them for quick meals or snacks. Chop your favorite raw vegetables every few days and keep them visible in your fridge to munch on. Make extra whenever you make rice, beans, soup, roasted vegetables, or salad dressings so you have something in the fridge ready to eat. Keep fruit on your counter so you'll see it and eat it. Keep nuts, seeds, and no-added-sugar dried fruit in your car so you have something healthy to eat away from home.

ABOUT THIS COOKBOOK

This cookbook is designed to get adults and kids cooking together. Recipes are given a skill level of 1, 2, or 3 based on the following chart. Children should make any recipe with an adult the first time, and with practice, they'll be a capable cook all on their own!

SKILL LEVEL 1: These recipes are best for the littlest cooks to do with help or for older kids to do on their own after guided practice.

SKILL LEVEL 2: Little ones will mostly watch; older kids can make these with help or on their own with practice. These recipes require little to no chopping.

SKILL LEVEL 3: These are kid-favorite recipes designed for adults and experienced teenagers to make. Younger chefs may help where able. These have no limit on ingredients or difficulty. Skills like dicing, using the blender, etc., are needed.

For detailed nutritional information for each recipe, scan the code or visit faithfulplateful.com/recipe-nutrition-information/

WHAT CAN KIDS DO?

*H*elp your child become a capable cook by teaching these skills as they grow! Every child has different circumstances that will influence their capabilities, but in general, it seems children ages 3-4 can learn to do the easy skills, ages 5-7 can learn the medium skills, and ages 8 and over can learn to do the hard skills.

EASY SKILLS

- Stir dry ingredients and batter
- Pour pre-measured ingredients into a bowl
- Mash bananas or cooked potatoes with a potato masher
- Spread nut butter
- Smell spices and ingredients and give an opinion
- Wipe up spills
- Push buttons on a blender or food processor
- Scoop ingredients with measuring cup or spoon
- Peel garlic and onions

- Cut soft things with a butter knife or kid's knife, like cooked potatoes or mushrooms.
- Make a fruit salad by cutting bananas, berries, pears, peeled kiwi, etc.
- Wash and tear lettuce
- Stand on a chair or stool and wash plastic containers and utensils in a sink of water
- Unload dishwasher and sort utensils
- Make Level 1 recipes with help

MEDIUM SKILLS

- Know knife safety
- Cut medium-density foods like zucchini, cucumbers
- Scoop cookie dough or muffin batter
- Drain and cut tofu
- Use a peeler for carrots or cucumbers
- Set the table and clear the table

- Wipe counters, table, and chairs
- Read basic recipes and make some by themselves
- Pack their own lunches (with guidance)
- Make Level 1 recipes on their own (after practice with an adult)
- Help with Level 2 and Level 3 recipes and make them on their own with time

HARD SKILLS

- Use a sharp knife
- Use small appliances on their own, like a blender and food processor
- Open cans
- Double or half a recipe
- Make decisions about adjusting a recipe or even make up their own
- Plan a meal by themselves
- Wash dishes

- Steam and sauté vegetables
- Boil and drain pasta
- Dice, mince, and chop all fruits and vegetables
- Make a weekly meal plan
- Create a shopping list based on a meal plan
- Shop within a budget
- Find their own recipes online

ALLERGIES

 Recipes that are naturally gluten-free, without altering the recipe, are labeled with this GF symbol. Recipes that use oats are considered naturally gluten-free. It is assumed you use certified gluten-free oats if you need the recipe to be gluten-free. It is also assumed you'll use gluten-free versions of ingredients such as soy sauce, ketchup, and vegetable broth if you have a gluten allergy.

 Recipes that are naturally nut-free, without altering the recipe, are labeled with this NF label.

Almost all the recipes that are NOT naturally free of these ingredients include alternate ingredients listed on the side to suit a gluten-free or nut-free diet.

Cashews

Cocoa Powder

Chocolate Chips

Flax Seeds

NUT ALLERGIES

Many of the recipes have either peanuts or tree nuts. When possible, there is a note indicating how to make a recipe nut-free. Almond flour is a whole-food ingredient that makes baked goods particularly tender and soft without using oil, so it is a common ingredient in this cookbook. However, there are listed options for substituting a nut-free alternative for the almond flour.

If you have a cashew allergy, you can substitute almonds or sunflower seeds for the cashews. The flavor might be slightly different, and the texture not quite as creamy, but it usually still tastes good. Blended-up sunflower seeds do turn foods a slightly green color. If you don't have a high-speed blender (like a Vitamix or Blendtec), soak any nuts or seeds first for at least a few hours (preferably overnight) before blending.

GLUTEN ALLERGIES

All the recipes in this book can be modified to be gluten-free, so there is no separate gluten-free section. For recipes that are not naturally gluten-free, there is a note at the side of each recipe indicating how to modify it. Make sure to use certified gluten-free oats in all the recipes if you have an allergy. Having gluten-free all-purpose flour and gluten-free oats to make oat flour will help.

NOTES ABOUT INGREDIENTS

- **CASHEWS**: Cashews are a common way to make things creamy in plant-based cooking. As mentioned earlier, if you do not have a high-speed blender (like a Vitamix or Blendtec), it is recommended to always soak cashews before blending them. You can do this quickly by boiling water, adding cashews, and letting them soak for at least 20 minutes. If you'd rather skip boiling water, you can soak cashews in room-temperature water for 2 hours instead. If you are allergic to cashews, refer to the Nut Allergies section above.

- **COCOA POWDER**: We refer to cocoa powder and cacao powder interchangeably. Cacao is made from raw cocoa beans, and cocoa is made from roasted cocoa beans. You can use either, as they taste pretty similar. It's best to find fair trade cacao powder for the most nutrients and to support fair cocoa harvesting practices.
- **CHOCOLATE CHIPS**: Unfortunately, there is no such thing as a chocolate chip tree, so chocolate chips are not a whole food. They fall into our 10% of processed food. Look for dairy-free semi-sweet or dark chocolate chips in bulk bins, or look for the following brands: Toll House Allergen-Free, Good & Gather Organic (Target brand), Simple Truth Organic (Kroger brand), Great Value Organic (Walmart brand), Lily's Sweets, Enjoy Life, or Guittard Semi-Sweet or Dark.
- **FLAX SEEDS**: Buy whole flax seeds and grind them yourself to get the most nutrition at the lowest cost. You can grind them in a small blender (like a Nutribullet) or a coffee grinder. Keep the ground flax in the freezer to preserve freshness and nutrition. I like to buy golden flax seed so it is less visible in food.
- **FLOURS**: You can easily make your own flours in a good blender. You can blend dry corn, wheat, chickpeas, etc., in a high-speed blender or wheat grinder.
- **OAT FLOUR**: Blend certified gluten-free oats in a blender for the simplest whole-grain, gluten-free oat flour. I use the same amount of oats as needed for flour (i.e., 1 cup rolled oats for 1 cup oat flour).
- **ALMOND FLOUR**: Blend almonds until very fine for almond flour (on low speed, and preferably with the other dry ingredients in the recipe so as to avoid making almond butter), or purchase almond flour made from blanched almonds (it has a preferable texture).
- **NUTRITIONAL YEAST**: This ingredient is made from deactivated yeast and gives a rich umami taste to dishes without using cheese. If you don't use it, miso paste or vegan cheese may be a good substitute in some recipes. It's best to use non-fortified and non-GMO brands, like Sari, which can be bought on Amazon.

Whole Wheat Flour

Oat Flour

Almond Flour

Nutritional Yeast

Plant Milk

Salt

Hemp Seeds

Pumpkin Seeds

- **OIL**: Oil is not a whole food. It is very high in fat and calories and is linked to numerous health complications. We try to use whole-food fats instead of oil, since whole foods (like avocados instead of avocado oil) contain fiber and more nutrition. However, if you prefer to use oil to sauté or roast vegetables or in the place of nut butter in baked goods to avoid nuts, you can certainly use oil however you please with these recipes. Children do need more fat than adults, and most experts agree that small amounts of minimally processed oils (such as olive or avocado oil on occasion) are not problematic if weight loss is not the goal. Although some fat is needed in a diet, no one needs saturated fat, so try to avoid coconut oil (and excessive amounts of full-fat coconut milk).

- **PLANT MILK**: When a recipe calls for plant milk, you can use any kind you have. Canned coconut milk is the highest in fat, so it makes things more indulgent and creamy (however, since it is high in saturated fat, it should be used sparingly). Soy milk is the next highest in fat, has the most protein, and is an excellent choice for creamy smoothies. We mostly use almond milk at our house, but cashew, oat, hemp, rice, pea—all the options!—will work. Make sure to buy unsweetened plant milk to avoid unnecessary sugar.

- **SALT**: Salt can be used sparingly in a whole-food, plant-based lifestyle. It is recommended to not consume more than 1,500 mg of sodium per day (about 1/2 teaspoon salt or one tablespoon of soy sauce). Salt is listed in the recipes in this book so they will taste normal to someone transitioning from a standard American diet, but you can always leave it out or reduce it if you prefer. If you are used to a lot of salt, it is best to sprinkle a little salt on your own serving right before eating it instead of adding lots of salt to an entire recipe and then adding *more* salt on top.

- **SEEDS**: Although seeds can be expensive, I urge you to make them a priority to buy. Ground flax seeds make a great egg replacement in baking and have incredible health benefits. Hemp seeds, pumpkin seeds, sunflower seeds, sesame seeds, and chia seeds should all be staples in your pantry for good nutrition. At our house, we call hemp seeds "sprinkles" and sprinkle them on fruit, oatmeal, and even Nice Cream (see page 170). Although hemp seeds are related to the marijuana plant, they do not contain any of the addictive drug compounds and are a safe and nutritious choice.

- **SOY SAUCE**: You can use any alternative to soy sauce if you prefer. Tamari (gluten-free soy sauce), coconut aminos, and Bragg Liquid Aminos are all good alternatives.

- **SWEETENERS**: You can use whatever sweetener you are accustomed to using with these recipes. We like to use maple syrup because it works very well in recipes and is a natural, whole food that comes straight from a tree. You can always substitute honey for maple syrup if you prefer; they work interchangeably.

Dates are healthier than any sugar or syrup, since they contain fiber and more nutrition. To make date paste, blend soaked dates with just enough water to make the blender go and run the blender until the paste is smooth. This can be used in the place of maple syrup in most recipes. The extra fiber will make the food a different texture, however.

Although sugar and brown sugar are not whole foods, they might sometimes be the only things available. Though not ideal, you can use sugar instead of maple syrup if needed. You may just need to add a little water. Coconut sugar is a lower-glycemic sweetener and can also be used. Monk fruit sweetener or stevia may also work, although they have not been tested in these recipes. Really, you can swap out the maple syrup listed in the recipe for whatever sweetener best meets your economic and dietary needs.

If you are avoiding sweeteners altogether (a beneficial choice!), you can often leave them out or replace them with mashed banana, applesauce, or date paste.

No sweetener is a health food. Try to use as few sweeteners as possible, and your taste buds

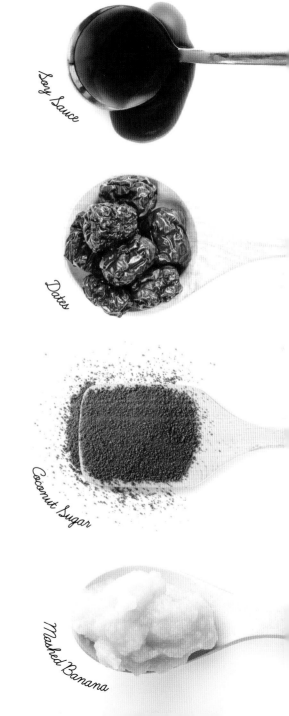

Soy Sauce

Dates

Coconut Sugar

Mashed Banana

Taco Seasoning

Tahini

Tofu

Vegetable Broth

will adjust. The recipes in this book are developed to be sweet enough for the average person while using the smallest amount possible, but you can adjust to your preference.

- **TACO SEASONING**: You can buy a premade seasoning, or make your own to keep in your cupboard:

  6 TBSP chili powder
  2 TBSP cumin
  2 TBSP garlic powder
  2 TBSP onion powder
  1 TBSP oregano
  1 TBSP paprika (or smoked paprika)
  1 TBSP salt
  1 TBSP pepper

  Mix together and keep in a jar. Make sure to label it.

- **TAHINI**: Tahini is just blended-up sesame seeds and is a staple ingredient in hummus. Tahini can have a strong flavor, so I sometimes use sunflower seed butter (sold next to peanut butter in most grocery stores) interchangeably with tahini. Adding an acid like lime or lemon juice also subdues the bitterness of tahini. Having tahini on hand is convenient. It adds creaminess and depth of flavor to the recipes that call for it. It is also a great option if you can't eat nuts. Try different brands if you feel your tahini is too bitter.

- **TOFU**: The wrong brand of tofu can make you not like tofu! Look for extra-firm or super-firm tofu. My favorite brands are Fountain of Health (often sold at Costco) and Nasoya Super Firm (at Walmart). You can also buy a tofu press to make softer brands more firm.

- **VEGETABLE BROTH**: The easiest and cheapest way to get vegetable broth is to buy a broth base that you mix with water instead of buying boxed or canned broth. We like Better than Bouillon Organic Vegetable Broth Base, available at most grocery stores in the soup aisle. Mix one teaspoon of the base with 1 cup water to make 1 cup of broth.

SHOULD I BUY ORGANIC INGREDIENTS?

I am not an expert on pesticides, and the topic is beyond the scope of this book. There is a dirty dozen list[10] that lists the produce with the most pesticides (mostly leafy greens, berries, apples, and other produce we eat the skin of). I personally try to buy organic wheat, corn, and soy products. If you can't afford organic, studies show that eating fruits and vegetables is beneficial regardless of whether they are organic or not. Don't let the fear of eating nonorganic produce keep you from stuffing your face with fruits and vegetables!

EQUIPMENT

In addition to basic kitchen tools like mixing bowls and knives, these other tools are highly recommended. You can find links to recommended products at faithfulplateful.com.

- High-speed blender
- Food processor
- Silicone muffin pan or silicone muffin liners (to avoid greasing pans)
- Silicone baking mat
- Lemon-squeezer
- Garlic press
- Cookie scoop
- Popsicle molds

KITCHEN SAFETY TIPS TO DISCUSS WITH YOUR CHILD

- Always ask permission before you start cooking. Make sure an adult is either helping you or nearby (even if you are doing all the work).
- Wash your hands before you begin cooking.
- Turn the pot handles away from the front of the stove so they can't be bumped off or pulled down by little children. Keep handles away from other hot burners so you don't burn your hand on them.
- Before you leave the kitchen after cooking, always make sure the oven and stove are turned off and small appliances are unplugged.
- Clean as you cook. It will help keep you safe from spills and falls.
- Never put sharp knives, graters, blades, or peelers into

METRIC CONVERSIONS

Customary	Metric
VOLUME	
1/4 teaspoon	1.25 ml
1/2 teaspoon	2.5 ml
1 teaspoon	5 ml
1 tablespoon	15 ml
1 fluid ounce	30 ml
1/4 cup	60 ml
1/3 cup	80 ml
1/2 cup	120 ml
1 cup	240 ml
1 pint	480 ml
1 quart	960 ml
1 gallon	3.84 L
WEIGHT	
1 ounce (weight)	28 g
1/4 pound	114 g
1 pound	454 g
TEMPERATURE	
250° F	120° C
300–325° F	150–160° C
325–350° F	160–175° C
350–375° F	175–190° C
375–400° F	190–205° C
400–450° F	205–230° C
450–500° F	230–260° C

KITCHEN CONVERSIONS

Dash	Less than 1/8 teaspoon
Pinch	About 1/8 teaspoon
1 cup	1/2 pint = 16 TBSP
1 TBSP	3 teaspoons
1/4 cup	4 TBSP
1/3 cup	5 TBSP + 1 teaspoon
1/2 cup	8 TBSP

a sink of soapy water. Wash them and put them directly into the dishwasher (pointed down) or put them away.

- Practice cutting with knives with an adult for a long time before you ever try cutting on your own.
- Make sure babies and toddlers are not nearby when you open the oven, so they don't reach in and burn themselves.
- Lift pot lids away from you, so the steam doesn't burn your face. Always use a potholder or oven mitt when you need to touch a hot pot or pan.
- Ask an adult to pour and blend hot foods in a blender. Hot foods in blenders can be very dangerous if the lid comes off.
- Keep long hair tied back.
- Read the recipe before you start cooking. Know what to expect.

COOKING BASICS & TERMS TO TEACH YOUR CHILD

- **OMIT**: This means to leave out an ingredient without replacing it with anything.
- **SAUTÉ**: In this cookbook, we water sauté as opposed to sautéing in oil. To water sauté, put the vegetables in a skillet. They will begin to release their own water, but once the pan begins to turn brown or the vegetables stick, add a few tablespoons of water. Stir and add small amounts of water until the vegetables are tender. Too much water will steam the vegetables, which doesn't create the same flavor as a sauté.

- **BOIL**: Fill a pot halfway with water. Put it on the burner on high heat with a lid. Once the water makes big rolling bubbles, it is boiling.
- **SIMMER**: A simmer is when liquids are just below boiling. It creates very small bubbles. For example, when making soup, you often bring it to a boil and then reduce the heat so the soup cooks at a simmer.
- **SLICE**: Slicing means cutting across the food to make thick or thin pieces that are all the same size.
- **CHOP**: Chopping means cutting food into bite-size pieces, usually about 1/4-inch size (about the thickness of a pencil). If it says "finely chopped," cut it about half that size. Use a chef's knife to chop and always practice with an adult until you've mastered it.
- **DICE**: Dicing is similar to a fine chop. It means cutting food into very small pieces (about 1/8-inch in size) so you don't bite into a big piece. Peppers, carrots, tomatoes, and potatoes are often diced.
- **MINCE**: Mincing is even smaller than dicing. You can dice with a chef's knife or use a food processor or even a grater. Garlic and ginger are often minced so that they give flavor but you don't taste a big chunk.

Mince

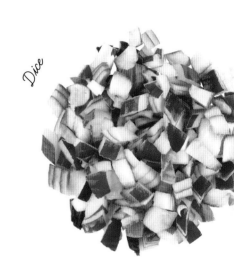

Dice

Slice

Chop

BREAKFAST

Variations

ALMOND GINGER
Use almond butter and add 2 tsp ground ginger or 2 TBSP freshly grated ginger root.

PEANUT BUTTER CHOCOLATE CHIP
Use peanut butter and add mini chocolate chips to cooled granola.

PIÑA COLADA
Omit cinnamon. Use almond butter and add shredded coconut and chopped dried pineapple, banana, and/or mango to cooled granola.

ORANGE CRANBERRY PECAN
Use chopped pecans for the nuts, add the zest of one large orange before baking, and add dried cranberries to cooled granola.

MAPLE SEA SALT
Use almond butter, 1/2 tsp maple extract, and a heaping 1/2 tsp of coarse salt instead of 1/2 tsp regular salt.

HOMEMADE
GRANOLA

Use your favorite nuts, seeds, and fruit to create your own version of delicious granola!

MAKES: 4 CUPS
SKILL LEVEL: 2
COOK TIME: 35 MINUTES

For nut-free, use tahini or sunflower butter instead of nut butter. Omit nuts and use additional seeds instead.

Ingredients

DRY
4 cups rolled oats
1/2 TBSP cinnamon
1/2 cup sunflower, pumpkin, or sesame seeds
1/2 cup chopped nuts (any kind)

WET
1/2 cup nut butter

1/2 cup maple syrup (or 3/4 cup date paste)
1 tsp vanilla or almond extract

ADD AT THE END
1/2 cup dried fruit (raisins, apricots, dates, dried apples, shredded coconut, or craisins)

NUTRITIONAL BENEFITS
Oats have protein, iron, and a special fiber called beta-glucan that lowers cholesterol.

Instructions

1. Preheat the oven to 325 degrees. Line a cookie sheet with parchment paper or a silicone baking mat.

2. Mix dry ingredients (except dried fruit) in a large bowl.

3. Mix nut butter, maple syrup, and extract together. Warm up in the microwave if needed to make it pourable.

4. Toss all together until everything is coated.

5. Spread onto the lined cookie sheet. Bake 20 minutes, then stir the granola and bake about 5-10 minutes more until golden brown and dry. Watch it carefully, as it burns easily.

6. Let cool completely, which helps it crisp up. Stir in dried fruit and store in a container, jars, or bag.

TIP

Cookies stay good for up to 2 days at room temperature, or frozen for up to 3 months.

To freeze, put cooled cookies in a sealed plastic bag. Take a few out and either let them sit on the counter for about 30 minutes, or microwave them for 10-20 seconds.

CARROT CAKE
BREAKFAST
COOKIES

For nut-free, omit almond butter.

NF

NUTRITIONAL BENEFITS
Carrots have beta carotene, which can improve your eye health.

Ingredients

DRY INGREDIENTS
1 cup oat flour
1 1/2 cups rolled oats
1 tsp baking powder
1/2 tsp salt
2 tsp cinnamon
1/4 tsp ground ginger
1/2 tsp allspice
1 cup grated carrots

1/4 cup raisins
2 TBSP hemp seeds (optional)

WET INGREDIENTS
3/4 cup applesauce
1/4 cup almond butter
1/3 cup maple syrup or date paste
2 TBSP ground flax seeds

Instructions

1   Preheat oven to 350 degrees and line a baking sheet with a silicone baking mat or parchment paper.

2   Stir the dry ingredients together, including the carrots, raisins, and hemp seeds.

3   In another bowl or liquid measuring cup, stir together the wet ingredients and flax seeds.

4   Stir all together and drop by spoonfuls onto the baking sheet (about 16-20 cookies).

5   Bake for 15 minutes.

6   Enjoy cooled cookies with a glass of plant milk! Cookies freeze well and thaw quickly for a fast breakfast, too.

The burritos can be wrapped in wax paper, packed together in a zip-top bag, and then frozen. To reheat, microwave one burrito in its wax-paper wrapping for 1-2 minutes.

BREAKFAST
BURRITOS

MAKES: 4-6 BURRITOS
SKILL LEVEL: 2
COOK TIME: 25 MINUTES

Tofu makes a really yummy breakfast burrito. Feel free to add any other ingredients you like; for example: black beans, bell pepper, spinach, cilantro, red onion, rice, or avocado.

For gluten-free, you can make these into tacos with corn tortillas or eat the filling all by itself!

Ingredients

2 medium potatoes
1 package extra-firm tofu
2 TBSP nutritional yeast
1/4 tsp turmeric
1 tsp garlic powder
1 tsp onion powder

3/4 tsp salt
Pepper to taste
6 whole-grain tortillas
For serving: Paprika Eureka Sauce (see page 136), salsa, avocado, chopped green onions, or hot sauce

Instructions

1. Bake the potatoes first. You can do this by microwaving them for about 7-9 minutes or by cooking them in the oven or pressure cooker beforehand (see page 111 for help on how to cook potatoes).

2. While the potatoes bake, open the tofu and put it into a cold skillet, including the liquid. Crumble the block of tofu into small pieces with a fork or your hands. Turn on heat to medium-high.

3. Sprinkle the nutritional yeast, turmeric, garlic powder, onion powder, and salt over the tofu. Mix until it's thoroughly coated and yellow and the liquid has cooked off. Season with black pepper. Remove from heat.

4. Chop the baked potatoes and mix them in. Add any other ingredients if you want, such as rice, beans, tomatoes, avocado, or cilantro.

5. Spoon some tofu mixture into the center of each tortilla, add any toppings you like (such as hot sauce or salsa), and wrap up. Enjoy!

NUTRITIONAL BENEFITS
Tofu is a great source of protein and calcium, which are important for kids as they grow. Tofu has more calcium than cow milk; cow milk has 120mg of calcium per 100 grams, but tofu has 350mg![11]

Blender Banana Oat Pancakes

MAKES 15-20 PANCAKES

These pancakes don't use a mix, but they are simple to make in your blender. They are my family's favorite pancakes!

INGREDIENTS

1 ripe banana

2 1/2 cups water or plant milk

1/2 cup chopped dates (optional)

3 cups rolled oats

2 TBSP baking powder

1 tsp vanilla extract (optional)

1/4 tsp salt

INSTRUCTIONS

1. In a large blender, blend all the ingredients together. (If using the dates, blend them with the water or milk together first until smooth, then add the rest of the ingredients.)

2. Let batter sit for a few minutes to thicken while a large skillet heats up to 350 degrees (medium-high).

3. Pour the batter into pancake shapes and cook. They are yummy even without any toppings. Keep extras in the fridge or freezer for snacks or breakfasts.

OPTIONAL: Blend in 1 cup wild blueberries for purple pancakes!

FLUFFY PANCAKE MIX

Ingredients

3 cups whole wheat flour, oat flour, spelt flour, or light buckwheat flour

3 TBSP baking powder

1 tsp salt

3/4 cup almond flour (optional—this will make more tender pancakes)

Instructions

TO MAKE THE MIX

1. Mix all ingredients together and pour into a jar or zip-top bag. Mix will store for about 3 months in a cool pantry, even with almond flour.

TO MAKE THE PANCAKES:

1. In a mixing bowl, gently stir together 1 cup of pancake mix with 1 cup of plant milk or water. Let batter rest for 5 minutes while your skillet heats up on medium-high.

2. Pour 1/3 cup of batter at a time on a hot skillet (if your skillet is not nonstick, grease it) and flip when bubbles appear.

3. Enjoy your fluffy, wholesome pancakes topped with applesauce, pure maple syrup, berries, nut butter, chopped nuts and seeds, and/or sliced bananas.

TIP
1 cup of pancake mix makes about 7 pancakes.

MAKES: 3 CUPS OF PANCAKE MIX OR 21 PREPARED PANCAKES
SKILL LEVEL: 1
COOK TIME: 5 MINUTES TO MAKE MIX; 20 MINUTES TO MAKE PANCAKES

For gluten-free, use light buckwheat flour or oat flour.

For nut-free, omit almond flour.

NUTRITIONAL BENEFITS

Eating whole grains will help prevent diseases like heart disease and Type 2 diabetes.

Variations

BANANA
Add 1 small mashed banana to the batter for each cup of mix.

LEMON
Add the zest of one lemon.

BLUEBERRY
Stir in 1/2 cup fresh or frozen blueberries.

Variations

BAKED PUMPKIN PANCAKES
Use pumpkin purée instead
of mashed banana, and use
pumpkin spice instead
of cinnamon. Top with
applesauce, chopped pears,
pecans, maple syrup, or even
Pumpkin Peanut Butter Dip
(see page 127).

Quick Berry Syrup

Make an easy berry sryup by
microwaving a bowl of frozen
berries and stirring in a
little maple syrup until it's
just sweet enough.

BAKED PANCAKES

Skip the flipping and standing over a skillet!.

Ingredients

DRY INGREDIENTS
3 cups rolled oats
1/4 cup whole or ground flax seeds
3 TBSP baking powder
1 tsp salt
1 TBSP cinnamon

WET INGREDIENTS
1 1/2 cups mashed banana (or pumpkin
   purée or applesauce)

1 1/2 cups plant milk
1 TBSP vanilla extract
1/4 cup maple syrup (optional, if you
   want it sweeter)

TOPPINGS
Maple syrup, berries, peanut butter,
   applesauce, and sliced bananas

NUTRITIONAL BENEFITS
Flax seeds have lignans,
which prevent cancer.[12] It's
recommended to eat flax
seeds every day!

Instructions

1. Preheat the oven to 400 degrees. Line a large rimmed cookie sheet with a silicone baking mat or parchment paper.

2. Put all the dry ingredients in a blender and blend into a fine flour. Pour the flour into a large bowl.

3. In the same blender that is now empty, add the banana, milk, and vanilla (and maple syrup, if using) and blend.

4. Pour the mixture into the bowl of dry ingredients and stir together (it is too thick to mix all of it in a blender, so definitely mix in the bowl).

5. Pour the batter into the pan and spread evenly with a rubber spatula. Bake for 20 minutes, or until a toothpick comes out clean.

6. Cool slightly. While still warm, cut into squares. Use a spatula and remove each piece, starting with the center so the pieces come out easier.

7. Serve with syrup, thawed frozen berries, peanut butter, applesauce, sliced bananas, or any other pancake topping.

TIP
Leftovers store well covered
in the fridge for about 3
days. You can also freeze
them in a sealed plastic bag
and reheat in the microwave
or toaster oven.

Variations

CHOCOLATE PEANUT BUTTER

Instead of berries and lemon juice, blend 2 TBSP cacao powder and 2 TBSP peanut butter with the milk and dates/maple syrup.

VANILLA

Omit the berries and lemon juice and include the vanilla extract instead.

TROPICAL

Blend 1 cup frozen pineapple and 1 cup frozen mango with 2 cups plant milk. Stir in 1/2 cup chia seeds and let thicken in the fridge.

BERRY YUMMY
CHIA PUDDING

Chia seeds swell up and transform milk into pudding!

Ingredients

2 cups plant milk

4 large, soft dates (or 1/4 cup maple syrup)

2 cups of your favorite berries (fresh or frozen)

2 TBSP freshly squeezed lemon juice

1 tsp vanilla extract (optional)

1/2 cup chia seeds

Optional toppings: fresh berries, nuts, seeds, and coconut

Instructions

1. Blend the milk, dates (or maple syrup), berries, lemon juice, and extract (if using) together in a blender.

2. Stir in the chia seeds. Taste and add more sweetener if you think it needs it.

3. Pour into a jar or container with a lid. Let it sit in the fridge for 4 hours, or overnight. It should be thick like yogurt or pudding, and seeds will be soft and no longer crunchy.

4. When ready to eat, top with more fresh berries, nuts, seeds, or coconut if you'd like. Enjoy!

NUTRITIONAL BENEFITS:
Chia seeds are an amazing source of protein, fiber, calcium, and magnesium, and help prevent constipation.

TIP

To store in the freezer, wrap
each bar in wax paper or
parchment paper, and freeze
in a sealed plastic bag. Let
them thaw for about 1 hour
or microwave for about 15
seconds.

BAKED OATMEAL BARS

Ingredients

WET
1 large, overripe banana (about 1/3 cup mashed)
1/3 cup maple syrup
1 cup plant milk or water
1/4 cup peanut butter

DRY
2 cups rolled oats
2 tsp baking powder
1 tsp cinnamon
1/2 tsp salt
2 TBSP ground flax seeds
Optional mix-ins: 1/2 cup chopped walnuts, frozen berries, raisins, or chocolate chips

Instructions

1. Preheat the oven to 350 degrees. Get out an 8x8-inch square baking pan. No need to grease it, but you can line it with parchment paper for easier cleanup if you want.

2. Mash the banana in a large bowl with a fork, then stir in the maple syrup, milk, and peanut butter. (Or, you can blend all that in a blender, then pour into the bowl.)

3. Stir in the dry ingredients.

4. Spread the mixture into the pan. If desired, sprinkle additional nuts, berries, coconut, or chocolate chips on top.

5. Bake for 35-40 minutes, until the center is firm. Let it cool for at least 15 minutes before cutting into squares. Eat them on their own or in a bowl with plant milk and fruit.

For nut-free, replace peanut butter with 1/4 cup applesauce, 1/4 cup extra mashed banana, or 1/4 cup sunflower seed butter.

Homemade Nutella

Nuts and seeds are some of the most nutrient-dense foods, and it's beneficial to eat some every day! Hemp seeds have lots of minerals and omega-3 fatty acids, which are very important for overall health. This homemade nutella is full of them!

INGREDIENTS

3/4 cup hemp seeds (or almonds or toasted hazelnuts)

4 large Medjool dates or 8 small dates

1/2 cup plant milk

1 1/2 TBSP cocoa powder

1 tsp pure vanilla extract

INSTRUCTIONS

1. Blend all ingredients together until smooth.

If you don't have a good blender, stir together these alternate ingredients: 1/2 cup almond or peanut butter, 1/4 cup maple syrup, 1 1/2 TBSP cocoa powder, and 1 tsp vanilla.

CREATIVE TOASTS

Ingredients

FOR SWEET

Whole-grain or gluten-free bread
Your favorite nut or seed butter or
   Homemade Nutella (see opposite)
Strawberries
Blueberries
Bananas
Raisins
Hemp seeds

FOR SAVORY

Whole-grain or gluten-free bread (we love
   sourdough)
Avocado or hummus (see page 115)
Tomatoes
Basil leaves
Olives
Cucumbers
Sprouts
Carrots
Sauerkraut
Peas
Salt and pepper

Instructions

FOR SWEET TOAST:

1. Wash the berries. Cut the strawberries into slices. Slice the banana.

2. Toast the bread, then spread it with your favorite nut or seed butter.

3. Use the toppings to make animal or silly faces. Use banana slices for eyes with blueberries or raisins for the pupils. Banana slices also make great bear or mouse ears. Use strawberry slices for the scales of a fish or pointy ears of a fox. Hemp seeds make good sprinkles. Be creative!

FOR SAVORY TOAST:

1. Spread mashed avocado or hummus on toasted bread. Sprinkle it with salt and pepper (smoked paprika or "everything bagel seasoning" are also delicious!).

2. Add cucumber, tomato, peas, carrots, olives, sauerkraut, or sprouts to decorate!

VEGGIE MORNINGS

Even though oatmeal, toast, smoothies, and pancakes are what we think of as the breakfast foods, vegetables are a great way to start your day. In fact, eating a non-starchy vegetable before any meal will keep you full for longer and give you better energy, since it prevents a stark spike and crash in blood sugar.[13] So, while you're making your breakfast, snack on a bell pepper, cucumber, stick of celery, or heat up some frozen peas. See if you notice a difference in how you feel!

TIP
To sweeten with dates
instead of maple syrup,
blend 1 cup dates with the
milk and combine with the
other ingredients. The
porridge will be more brown,
but delicious.

THE THREE BEARS' OVERNIGHT PORRIDGE

MAKES: 6-8 SERVINGS
SKILL LEVEL: 1
TOTAL TIME: 10 MINUTES OF PREP, THEN OVERNIGHT

GF NF

Make this before going to bed, and you'll have a yummy, creamy breakfast (kind of like rice pudding) waiting for you in the morning! Be careful if you go for a walk while it cools. . . . Goldilocks can't resist this stuff.

Ingredients

PORRIDGE

1 cup uncooked brown rice, farro, or oat groats

1 cup water if using Instant Pot; 3 cups water if using slow cooker

1 1/2 cups almond milk

1 can light coconut milk (or 1 1/2 cups additional almond milk for lower fat)

1/2 tsp salt

1/2 cup maple syrup

1 tsp cinnamon

1/4 tsp nutmeg

1 tsp vanilla

1/4 cup raisins (optional)

TOPPINGS

Fresh bananas or other fruit, plant milk, maple syrup, or chopped nuts

Instructions

1. Before going to bed, combine all porridge ingredients in a slow cooker or Instant Pot. (If you don't like plumped raisins, don't add them until the morning.)

2. In a slow cooker, cook on low for 6 hours. In the Instant Pot, set to high pressure for 30 minutes and push the "Keep Warm" button. It will naturally release the pressure overnight and keep the porridge warm until morning.

3. In the morning, serve porridge with sliced bananas, fresh or frozen berries, more milk, and a drizzle of maple syrup. Sprinkle with chopped nuts or seeds if you'd like a little crunch. It can be eaten hot or cold.

You can also use millet, steel-cut oats, or buckwheat as the grain. Consistency and flavor will vary.

**MAKES: 1 LARGE SMOOTHIE
OR 2-3 SMALL ONES
SKILL LEVEL: 1
PREP TIME: 10 MINUTES**

Un-Beet-Able Hot Pink Smoothie

Pretty soon, you won't need a recipe for smoothies—you'll know what ingredients you like and will make up your own combinations. For now, here are some of our favorites!

Un-Beet-Able Hot Pink Smoothie

Beets are very good for your heart because of their high nitrate levels, which lower blood pressure. Or, should we say, good for your heart-"beet?"[14]

BLEND TOGETHER:

- 12 frozen strawberries
- 1 small beet (2-3 inches in diameter), peeled and sliced
- 3 pitted dates or 1 banana
- 1 TBSP cashews or hemp seeds
- 1 1/2 cups plant milk
- Optional: Add 2 TBSP cocoa for a chocolate beet smoothie!

Lucky Green Smoothie

Lucky for you, this green smoothie is super yummy and boosts your immune system!

BLEND TOGETHER:

- 1 cup frozen pineapple or mango
- 1 cup frozen banana chunks
- 1/4 cup frozen orange juice concentrate or 1 peeled orange
- 2 packed cups fresh spinach
- 2 cups water
- 1 thumb-size piece of fresh ginger root (optional)
- 1 TBSP hemp seeds (optional)

Lucky Green Smoothie

Cruciferous Chocolate Peanut Butter Smoothie

Cruciferous vegetables are especially good at preventing disease. They contain a powerful phytochemical called sulforaphane, which protects your cells. Some cruciferous vegetables include broccoli, cauliflower, Brussels sprouts, cabbage, kale, and bok choy. It benefits us to eat some of these vegetables every day!

BLEND TOGETHER:

1/2 cup frozen cauliflower (riced or florets)

1 large, overripe frozen banana (about 2 cups frozen banana chunks)

1 1/4 cups plant milk

1 TBSP cocoa powder

1-2 TBSP peanut butter or peanut butter powder (or other nut/seed butter)

1-2 dates (optional, for extra sweetness)

Cruciferous Chocolate Peanut Butter Smoothie

Orange Julius Smoothie

BLEND TOGETHER:

1/3 cup frozen orange juice concentrate

1 banana (optional)

1-2 TBSP maple syrup or honey

1 cup ice

1/2 cup plant milk

1 orange, peeled

1 tsp vanilla extract

1/2 cup diced yellow squash

Orange Julius Smoothie

Plant-Based "Parm"

Make this parmesan "cheese" to sprinkle on your potatoes before baking for cheesy potatoes. It's also yummy on pasta, soup, or salad.

INGREDIENTS

3/4 cup almond flour (or ground cashews, almonds, sunflower seeds, or hemp seeds)

1/4 cup nutritional yeast

1 TBSP italian seasoning (optional)

1/2 tsp salt

1/4 tsp garlic powder

INSTRUCTIONS

1. Combine all the ingredients in a jar and shake together.

2. Store in a jar. Keeps at room temperature for up to a month, or in the fridge for longer freshness. Sprinkle on potatoes, pasta, soup, or anything else you'd normally top with parmesan cheese.

46

SMASHED POTATOES

No chopping here, but smashing!

Ingredients

12 small Yukon Gold or red potatoes (about 2 pounds)

2 TBSP olive oil or aquafaba (liquid from a can of chickpeas)

Salt and pepper

Optional: Garlic powder, onion powder, rosemary, or Plant-Based "Parm" (see opposite)

Instructions

1. Scrub the potatoes and place them in a large pot. Cover the potatoes with 1 inch of water and set on the stove.

2. Bring the water to a boil. Let potatoes boil for about 20-25 minutes (depending on the size) until fork-tender.

3. While the potatoes cook, preheat the oven to 425 degrees and get out a large baking sheet. Line the baking sheet with parchment paper or a silicone baking mat. Set a large colander in the sink.

4. When the potatoes are done, drain them in the colander, being careful of the steam. Let them cool slightly or run some cold water over them so they aren't burning hot.

5. Using some tongs or an oven mitt to protect your hands, place the potatoes on the baking sheet. Use the bottom of a cup to press down on each potato and smash them, until they are about 1/2 inch or 1/4 inch thick (about the thickness of a marker or pencil).

6. Brush on oil or aquafaba with a pastry brush or your fingers. Use an oil-sprayer for oil if you have one. The potatoes will still be delicious without any oil or aquafaba, just not as crispy. Shake some salt and pepper on the potatoes. A sprinkle of garlic and onion powder or rosemary is also yummy, or sprinkle some Plant-Based "Parm" (see opposite) over them.

7. Place potatoes in the oven and set the timer for 25 minutes. Check them to see if they are brown and crispy. If not, bake for 5-10 more minutes.

8. Once cool enough to eat, enjoy with Paprika Eureka Sauce (see page 136), ketchup, pesto, or on their own.

NUTRITIONAL BENEFITS
Potatoes have lots of fiber, which keeps you feeling full. They also have a lot of potassium, one of the most vital minerals in your body. Potassium helps move nutrients into your cells, helps your heartbeat stay regular, supports healthy blood pressure, and allows your nerves to function and your muscles to contract.

A GUIDE TO COOKING OATMEAL

Whole grains make a perfect breakfast because they are yummy and keep you full for a long time. There are so many you can try! Buckwheat, amaranth, kamut, einkorn, quinoa, polenta, freekah, teff, brown rice, millet, farro, sorghum, and wheat berries, just to name some. On this page, however, you'll find a variety of ways you can easily prepare the most popular breakfast grain: oats. Other grains cannot be substituted for these instructions, but you can do quick internet searches to find out how to cook any grain if you'd like to try something new.

 A NOTE ON MEASUREMENTS: When it says "1 part oats and 2 parts water," that means you can use whatever measurement you want to! If you're making enough for one person, 1/2 cup could be your 1 part, and so 2 parts would be two 1/2 cups (1 cup). If you're making enough for a whole family, 2 cups oats could be your one part, and so 4 cups would be two parts.

 A NOTE ON SALT: Adding a little salt can make oats less bland, although if you're adding other flavorings, you may not notice and can reduce sodium consumption by leaving it out. If desired, add about 1/8 tsp salt (a pinch) per 1/2 cup oats.

METHOD	ROLLED OATS	STEEL-CUT OATS
STOVE TOP	Boil 2 parts water and then add 1 part rolled oats. Remove from heat, cover with lid, and let sit for 10-15 minutes until all the water is absorbed.	In a saucepan, bring 4 cups of water to a boil. Add 1 cup of steel-cut oats and reduce to a simmer. Let simmer uncovered, stirring occasionally, until oats are tender and liquid is absorbed (about 30-40 minutes). Be nearby to make sure it doesn't burn.
MICROWAVE A SINGLE SERVING	Put 1/2 cup rolled oats in a bowl and cover with 3/4 cup water. Microwave 1 minute, check on it, then 1 minute more.	Put 1/2 cup steel-cut oats and 2 cups water into a large microwave-safe bowl. The bowl needs to be able to hold 8 cups of water, because it will bubble up a lot. Microwave for 5 minutes, stir, and microwave 5 more minutes.

OVERNIGHT REFRIGERATED	Combine 1 part rolled oats with 1 1/2 parts milk or water in a bowl or jar with other ingredients (like fruit, nut butter, or maple syrup). Cover and let sit overnight in the fridge. In the morning, eat cold or warm it up. Lasts up to 5 days in the fridge. Serves 2-3 people for every 1 cup of oats.	Combine 1 part steel-cut oats with 1 3/4 parts milk and any other ingredients you'd like (fruit, nut butter, maple syrup, or chia seeds). Cover and let it sit overnight in the fridge. In the morning, eat cold or warm it up. Lasts up to 5 days in the fridge. Serves 4.
OVERNIGHT SLOW COOKER	This makes very creamy oatmeal! Before bed, put the following into a slow cooker: • 6 cups water • 2 cups rolled oats • 1/2 cup coconut milk (optional) Cook for 8 hours on the low setting of a slow cooker. Makes 3-4 servings.	Before bed, put this into a slow cooker: • 1 1/2 cups steel-cut oats • 6 cups water Cook on low for 8 hours. Makes 3-4 servings.
INSTANT POT	Add 1 part rolled oats and 1 1/2 parts plant milk or water to the Instant Pot. Cook on high pressure for 3 minutes. When it beeps, move the valve to the venting position for a quick release (stand back from the hot steam!). Once it's stopped steaming, you can open the lid and stir. Makes 3-4 servings.	Add 1 part steel-cut oats and 2 parts water into the Instant Pot. Let cook on high pressure for 4 minutes, then let it sit for 20 minutes to do a natural release. It will say LO:20.
OVERNIGHT STOVE TOP	Before going to bed, boil 2 parts water and then add 1 part rolled oats. Turn off the heat, cover with a lid, and in the morning it will be all cooked! Turn the stove back on to warm it up, if desired. (It is safe to eat because they are covered and are not at room temperature very long after cooling.)	Before going to bed, boil 3 parts water and add 1 part steel-cut oats. Turn off the heat, cover with a lid, and in the morning it will be all cooked! Turn the stove back on to warm it up, if desired.

After cooking oatmeal the way you choose, add flavor and sweetness! Check out page 50 for tons of ideas on how to flavor your oatmeal. Everyone can add their own toppings to their bowl, or you can flavor the whole pot so everyone can spoon out a ready-to-eat portion.

25+ WAYS TO FLAVOR YOUR OATMEAL

Plain cooked oatmeal is like a blank canvas, and you are the artist! You can add whatever combination of ingredients you like. Experiment to find your favorites!

- **ADD SWEETENER** to your oatmeal first, like some maple syrup, honey, or chopped dates.
- **PB&J:** chia jam or berries swirled with peanut butter
- **CINNAMON RAISIN SWIRL:** cinnamon, raisins, walnuts, and dates
- **BLUEBERRY CHEESECAKE:** fresh or frozen blueberries with nondairy yogurt
- **LEMON POPPYSEED:** lemon juice, lemon zest, and chia or poppy seeds
- **CHERRY GARCIA:** fresh or frozen cherries, chocolate chips, and shredded coconut
- **PEANUT BUTTER BANANA:** sliced bananas and peanut butter
- **CHOCOLATE-COVERED STRAWBERRY:** cocoa powder, vanilla, fresh or frozen strawberries on top, and chocolate chips
- **BAKED APPLE:** chopped or grated apple, cinnamon, vanilla, walnuts, raisins, and coconut
- **GOOD OLD RAISINS AND PEANUTS:** just like it sounds
- **TROPICAL PARADISE:** fresh or frozen mango, pineapple, shredded coconut, almonds
- **ALMOND JOY:** chopped almonds, shredded coconut, and chocolate chips or cocoa powder
- **STRAWBERRIES AND CREAM:** fresh or frozen berries and nondairy yogurt or plant milk
- **LEMON BLUEBERRY:** lemon juice, lemon zest, blueberries, and nondairy yogurt

- **PUMPKIN PECAN:** pumpkin pie spice, chopped pecans, and 1 TBSP pumpkin purée
- **PEANUT BUTTER CUP:** peanut butter and chocolate chips
- **BANANA NUT:** banana slices, walnuts, cinnamon, and nutmeg
- **GINGERBREAD COOKIE:** a sprinkle of nutmeg, ginger, cinnamon, and cloves
- **BANANA COCONUT CREAM PIE:** banana slices, coconut milk, and shredded coconut
- **PEANUT BUTTER COOKIE:** peanut butter, vanilla, and cinnamon
- **CARROT CAKE:** shredded carrots, pecans, raisins, coconut, and vanilla
- **PEACHES AND CREAM:** fresh or canned peaches, non-dairy yogurt or milk, cinnamon, and cloves
- **ALMOND BUTTER CHOCOLATE CHIP:** almond butter and chocolate chips
- **MINT BROWNIE:** cocoa powder, a drop of peppermint extract or essential oil, and chocolate chips
- **SUPERFOOD BOWL:** hemp seeds, chia seeds, ground flax seeds, walnuts, pumpkin seeds, and berries
- **TRAIL MIX:** peanuts, raisins, chocolate chips, dried apricots, and dates
- **RED, WHITE, AND BLUE:** fresh or frozen strawberries, blueberries, and sliced bananas

LUNCH

Box Mac 'N' "Cheese" Mix

INGREDIENTS

3/4 cup
nutritional
yeast

1/2 cup flour*

1 TBSP paprika
(not smoked)

2 tsp salt

2 tsp onion
powder

1 tsp garlic
powder

2 tsp lemon
pepper

1 TBSP coconut
sugar
(optional)

1/2 tsp
turmeric

INSTRUCTIONS

1. Stir all ingredients
together. Store the mix in a
labeled jar in the cupboard
or pantry. Lasts at least 3
months.

*Anything that thickens will work! Gluten-
free all-purpose flour, spelt flour, very
fine oat flour, whole wheat flour, brown
rice flour, cornstarch, or arrowroot
powder.

BOX MAC 'N' "CHEESE"

This is the quickest mac and "cheese" and it's so yummy! It doesn't taste exactly like store-bought boxed mac and cheese, but it also doesn't have the harmful chemicals of processed cheese mixes.

Ingredients

1 box (8 oz) whole-grain or legume pasta

2 cups plant milk

1/2 cup Box Mac 'n' "Cheese" Mix (see opposite)

1 TBSP cashew butter or vegan butter (optional)

Salt and pepper

Instructions

1. Boil 8 ounces of pasta according to package directions. Drain in a colander.

2. In the hot, empty pot, whisk 2 cups plant milk and 1/2 cup "cheese" mix together.

3. Turn the heat onto medium-low. Whisk and cook 2-5 minutes until thick and bubbling. Add 1 tablespoon cashew butter if you'd like.

4. Stir in the cooked pasta. Add more salt and pepper to taste.

DID YOU KNOW?
Whole-grain pasta contains more fiber and nutrients than white pasta. It will help you stay full for longer, even though it contains fewer calories than white pasta.

NF For nut-free, use nut-free plant milk like soy or pea milk.

GF For gluten-free, use gluten-free pasta such as brown rice or chickpea pasta.

NUTRITIONAL BENEFITS
Nutritional yeast contains certain carbohydrates called beta-glucan and alpha-mannan that boost your immune system and help you avoid sickness.

A NOTE ABOUT FIBER

The more variety of plants you eat, the wider variety of fiber you'll have to feed the different types of healthy microbes in your gut. A healthy gut will help you feel happier mentally and make your tummy feel good!

CHICKPEA SALAD
SANDWICHES

These sandwiches are even *better* than a tuna salad or chicken salad sandwich! I don't usually like tahini, but you can't even taste it here, and it adds creaminess without using mayo.

For gluten-free, you can wrap the chickpea salad in a large leaf of lettuce, or use gluten-free bread or tortillas.

Ingredients

SAUCE
2 TBSP tahini (or sunflower seed butter)
1 tsp Dijon mustard
1 TBSP maple syrup
1/4 tsp salt
1/4 tsp black pepper
1 TBSP lemon juice or cider vinegar
1 TBSP water

SANDWICH FILLING
1 can (15 oz) chickpeas, rinsed and drained
1/4 cup diced red onion
1/4 cup diced celery
1/4 cup diced pickle
1/4 cup finely chopped red grapes, apple, or dried cranberries

FOR SERVING
Bread, tomato, pickles, mustard, and lettuce

NUTRITIONAL BENEFITS
Chickpeas are very good for your gut health. They contain both soluble and insoluble fiber, and fiber feeds the healthy bacteria that our guts need.

Instructions

1 Mix the sauce ingredients together in a large bowl (or a food processor).

2 Add the chickpeas. Smash all the chickpeas with a fork against the sides of the bowl (or pulse in a food processor until mostly mashed).

3 Stir in the remaining filling ingredients.

4 Make a sandwich with bread and chickpea salad. Add any toppings you like, such as tomato, pickles, lettuce, or mustard.

Simple Honey Mustard Sauce

INGREDIENTS

1/4 cup Dijon mustard

1/4 cup honey or maple syrup

INSTRUCTIONS

1. Stir together and enjoy as a dip or on burgers.

CHICKPEA NUGGETS

Make these in big batches to freeze so you can put them in the oven or air fryer for a quick lunch.

Ingredients

2 cans (or 3 cups) chickpeas (not drained)

1 cup rolled oats

1 TBSP garlic powder

1 TBSP onion powder

1 tsp salt

1/4 tsp black pepper

1/2 tsp smoked paprika

2 TBSP tahini

2 cups whole-grain or gluten-free breadcrumbs, crushed cornflakes, or finely shredded unsweetened coconut

Instructions

1. Preheat the oven to 450 degrees or get out your air fryer.

2. Collect the liquid from the cans of chickpeas by draining them over a bowl. This liquid is called *aquafaba* (which means "water from beans").

3. Put the oats, spices, and tahini in a food processor and blend until the oats are fine like flour. Add the chickpeas and 1/4 cup of aquafaba and pulse the food processor just until mixed. Some texture is best; don't process it totally smooth. Add a little more aquafaba if the food processor struggles, or if the mixture is too dry to hold together.

4. Make a station with the chickpea mixture, a bowl of breadcrumbs, and a baking tray lined with parchment paper.

5. Using a cookie scoop if you have one, or just your hands, form little balls (about 1 heaping

tablespoon) of chickpea mixture and slightly flatten them. Coat them in the breadcrumbs. If the breadcrumbs don't stick well, dip them in aquafaba first, then breadcrumbs. This will make about 25-30 nuggets.

6 Bake in the oven for 30 minutes or in an air fryer at 400 degrees for 15-20 minutes. They taste good all by themselves, or eat them with ketchup, BBQ sauce, or Simple Honey Mustard Sauce (see opposite).

MAKES: 25-30 NUGGETS
SKILL LEVEL: 2
TOTAL TIME: 50 MINUTES

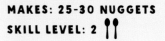

NUTRITIONAL BENEFITS
Chickpeas have lots of protein, fiber, iron, and B vitamins, like folate.

TIP
You can freeze unbaked nuggets ahead of time on a baking sheet and then transfer them to a bag. Keep the bag in the freezer; then, for a quick meal, put some frozen nuggets into an air fryer for 10-15 minutes or in the oven at 450 for 40-45 minutes until golden brown and crispy.

THE RIGHT TOFU

If you don't like tofu, it might be because you've only tried soft kinds. Look for extra-firm or super-firm varieties (sometimes also called "high-protein tofu"). If it is still too soft for your liking, press it by taking it out of the package and wrapping it in a kitchen towel. Set a heavy pot on top for 30-60 minutes. If you eat tofu often, you might want to buy a tofu press instead.

CRISPY TOFU

Why did the tofu cross the road? To prove it wasn't chicken!

Ingredients

1 block (12 oz) extra-firm tofu
1 TBSP soy sauce
1 tsp garlic powder

2 TBSP nutritional yeast (or cornstarch)

Instructions

1. If your tofu does not seem firm enough for your liking, press it (see opposite). Most extra-firm tofu does not need to be pressed.

2. Preheat the oven to 425 degrees or use an air fryer.

3. Line a baking sheet with a silicone baking mat or parchment paper. This is important for keeping the tofu crispy!

4. Cut the tofu into rows and then 1/2-inch cubes or rectangles. Put them in a bowl.

5. Pour the soy sauce over the tofu and stir very gently. Add the garlic powder and nutritional yeast and toss gently to coat all of the cubes.

6. Spread the cubes onto the baking sheet and bake for about 30 minutes, until brown and crispy. (Or cook in the air fryer at 370 degrees for 8-10 minutes, shaking every few minutes.)

7. Enjoy the tofu on its own, dipped in Peanut Sauce (see page 140), or in a Stir-Fry (see page 93).

Guacamole

INGREDIENTS

1 ripe avocado

Salt, pepper, and garlic powder to taste

1 lime

Salsa (optional)

INSTRUCTIONS

1. Cut the avocado in half from top to bottom, then scoop out the pit with a spoon. Use the spoon to remove the fruit from the skin into a bowl, then mash it with a fork.

2. Add a dash of salt, pepper, garlic powder, and a squeeze of lime juice.

3. Add a few tablespoons of salsa if you like. Taste and adjust until it's just right.

BEAN
"QUESADILLAS"

MAKES: 4 QUESADILLAS
SKILL LEVEL: 2
TOTAL TIME: 10 MINUTES

For gluten-free, use corn tortillas or gluten-free tortillas.

Ingredients

1 can (16 oz) fat-free refried beans
4–5 whole-grain tortillas
Salsa
Guacamole (see opposite)

FOR BUTTERFLY
Baby tomatoes, olives, or grapes
1 carrot, peeled and cut into thin, 1-inch sticks
Long skewers

Instructions

1. Open the can of beans and spread some on half of a tortilla. (Mixing 1/2 cup corn, a can of green chilies, or a teaspoon of Taco Seasoning—see page 20—in with the beans is also yummy.) Fold the tortilla over to create a half-circle.

2. Heat a skillet on medium heat. Cook the quesadilla until golden and crisp on each side. Remove it with a spatula to a plate.

3. Using a large knife or pizza cutter, cut each quesadilla in half to create two triangles.

4. Create the butterfly body by sliding several baby tomatoes, whole olives, or grapes onto a skewer. Place it in the middle of a plate and add two thin carrot sticks on top for antennae. Add two quesadilla triangles for wings.

5. Serve with salsa and/or guacamole and enjoy!

NUTRITIONAL BENEFITS

The groups of people who live the longest all have this in common: they eat beans every day! Many experts recommend that kids and adults eat beans or lentils every day.[15] Beans keep your blood sugar stable for a long time, help your gut bacteria to flourish, and provide a lot of the vitamins and minerals we need each day. Many experts, such as Joel Fuhrman, Michael Greger, and even the U.S. Dietary Guidelines, recommend both kids and adults eat an average of at least 1/2 cup of beans or lentils every day.

JACKFRUIT SUBSTITUTION

You can make these with a can of jackfruit, drained and shredded, instead of sweet potato. Sauté it in a skillet and then cover with BBQ sauce. Crumbled tofu or tempeh are other options that can be prepared the same way.

TIP

If you like a little more texture in your filling, all of these filling ingredients can be spread on a baking sheet and baked at 400 degrees for about 35 minutes (check frequently) until slightly crisped.

THREE-INGREDIENT BBQ SWEET POTATO SANDWICHES

MAKES: 4 LARGE SANDWICHES
SKILL LEVEL: 2 🍴🍴
TOTAL TIME: 15 MINUTES

For gluten-free, use certified gluten-free buns.

Ingredients

2 medium orange sweet potatoes or yams
Salt and pepper
1–2 cups BBQ sauce, plus extra for serving

4 whole-grain sandwich buns
Optional toppings: Shredded cabbage or pickles

Instructions

1. Peel the sweet potatoes (or don't—the skins have lots of nutritious fiber). Use 1 potato for every 2 sandwiches you want to make (it might seem like a lot, but the grated sweet potato shrinks quite a bit as it cooks).

2. Grate the sweet potatoes with a grater or a food processor attachment.

3. Cook in a skillet on medium-high heat, adding small amounts of water every minute or so, until the sweet potatoes look soft but not mushy. Season with salt and pepper.

4. Remove from heat, add BBQ sauce over it, and coat well. Toast the buns in the toaster on low.

5. Serve on a whole-grain bun with additional BBQ sauce and cabbage and/or pickles if desired.

TIP
Look for BBQ sauce that has 5 g of sugar or less per serving and no corn syrup. You can also make your own (see below).

Simple BBQ Sauce

INGREDIENTS

1 cup low-sugar ketchup
1/4 cup cider vinegar
3 TBSP pure maple syrup

2 TBSP soy sauce
1 TBSP smoked paprika
1 TBSP garlic powder

INSTRUCTIONS

1. Mix all ingredients together.

Instant Pot Version

INSTRUCTIONS

1. Combine all the ingredients except peas in the Instant Pot and set to high pressure for 20 minutes for brown rice, 12 minutes for white. Do a quick or natural release.

2. Add frozen peas and salt and pepper to taste.

3. Sprinkle with toppings if you'd like.

TIP

This is an easy make-ahead dinner or lunch, since it keeps well as leftovers. Make it even easier by using a bag of frozen riced cauliflower to save time chopping!

CURRIED RICE WITH VEGGIES

Ingredients

1 small onion, finely diced (about 3/4 cup)

2 cloves garlic, minced

2 carrots, quartered and chopped small (about 1 cup)

1 TBSP grated fresh ginger (or 1/2 tsp ground ginger)

1 TBSP curry powder

1 tsp coriander

1 tsp cumin

2 tsp salt

2 cups finely chopped or riced cauliflower (fresh or frozen)

1 1/2 cups uncooked brown basmati rice (or your favorite rice)

1 cup water

1 can (15 oz) petite diced tomatoes

3/4 cup canned coconut milk (full-fat or light) or soy milk

1 cup frozen peas

FOR SERVING

Optional toppings: Slivered almonds, cashews, dried cranberries, and cilantro

Instructions

1. Chop the onion, garlic, and carrots.

2. In a pot on the stove, sauté the onion, garlic, carrots, and ginger in a splash of water for about 5 minutes, until the onions start to look tender. Add the curry powder, coriander, cumin, and salt.

3. Add the cauliflower, rice, water, diced tomatoes, and coconut milk. Stir.

4. Bring to a boil, then turn heat down to low and let it simmer for 35–45 minutes for brown rice or about 20 minutes for white rice. Set a timer so it does not burn.

5. Stir in the frozen peas. Add more salt and pepper to taste. Sprinkle with toppings if you'd like. It will become less runny as it cools.

NUTRITIONAL BENEFITS
Ginger, garlic, and cauliflower help fight sickness. Garlic and ginger have potent antiviral, antibacterial, antioxidant, and anti-inflammatory properties. This means they are good at helping your immune cells fight sickness! Cauliflower also has high amounts of vitamin C and sulforaphane, which boost your immune system.

Homemade Creamy Italian Dressing

INGREDIENTS

1/2 cup raw
cashews,
slivered
almonds, or
sunflower
seeds
(soaked in
hot water
at least 20
minutes,
then
drained)

1/2 cup water

1 TBSP red
wine
vinegar

2 TBSP fresh
lemon juice

1 tsp maple
syrup

1/2 tsp garlic
powder

1/4 tsp each
salt and
pepper

1 TBSP Italian
seasoning
blend (or 1
tsp oregano,
1 tsp basil,
and 1 tsp
thyme)

INSTRUCTIONS

1. Blend ingredients together
   in a high-speed blender
   until very smooth.

PASTA SALAD

GF NF

Ingredients

2 cups dry whole-grain or legume pasta

1 cup broccoli, cut into small florets

1 cucumber, peeled and cubed

1 cup chopped tomatoes

1 small can sliced olives (optional)

1/2 cup Homemade Creamy Italian Dressing (see opposite) or use 1/2 cup of your favorite Italian dressing

Salt, pepper, and lemon juice (optional)

Instructions

1 Cook the pasta according to package directions and add the broccoli to the boiling water for the last 5 minutes. Drain in a colander and rinse in cold water to cool.

2 Chop the cucumber and tomato.

3 Add the cooked pasta and broccoli, cucumber, tomato, olives, and dressing to a large bowl and toss well. Season with salt, pepper, and lemon juice (optional) until it tastes just right to you. Keep refrigerated. Packs well for lunch!

NF

To make the dressing nut-free, omit the nuts and water and replace with 1/2 cup olive oil, aquafaba, or white beans.

GF

For gluten-free, use gluten-free pasta such as brown rice or chickpea pasta.

DID YOU KNOW?
Broccoli has vitamin K and calcium, both of which help you have strong bones and teeth.

SUSHI BOWLS OR ROLLS

You can keep everything separate (bento box style) or mix it all together with rice and soy sauce. Or, roll it up in a nori sheet and make sushi rolls!

Ingredients

1 cup dry, short-grain brown rice

1 cup frozen peas or edamame (for bowls)

1 sweet potato

1 cucumber, peeled

1 red bell pepper

1 mango

1 avocado

8 nori sheets (seaweed sheets—you can find these in the Asian aisle)

Soy sauce (or alternative like tamari, coconut aminos, or Bragg Liquid Aminos)

Optional: Spicy Cashew Mayo (see opposite)

Instructions

1. Cook the brown rice by putting 6 cups of water in a large pot, bringing it to a boil, and then adding the rice. Cover, reduce the heat to medium-low, and set a timer for 45 minutes. When cooked, drain excess water off and let sit until ready to eat. Using this much water helps eliminate common toxins in the rice.

2. If making bowls, thaw out the frozen peas or edamame in a bowl of water. (You won't use these if you're making rolls, since they are too big.)

3. Cook the sweet potato by placing it in the microwave for 5–8 minutes, depending on how big it is. Let it cool enough to handle.

4. Cut the sweet potato, cucumber, bell pepper, and mango into cubes if you're making sushi bowls. Cut them into thin strips if you're making rolls. Cut the avocado in half, remove the pit, then cut strips down each half. Use a spoon to scoop the pieces out of the skin.

5. Put all the fruits and vegetables on a plate or in individual bowls, them begin assembly.

Assembly

FOR BOWLS

1. Let everyone assemble their plate or bowl with rice and all the toppings.

2. Top with soy sauce or spicy mayo.

FOR ROLLS

1. Place a nori sheet on the counter.

2. Spread rice across it in a thin layer, leaving about an inch at the top uncovered.

3. Lay a thin strip of cucumber, bell pepper, sweet potato, avocado, and mango across the middle, then slowly roll it up. You may not be able to fit everything into every roll.

4. Dip your fingers in a bowl of water and get the top edge of the nori sheet wet, then seal it closed.

5. Cut the roll into slices with a serrated knife.

6. Use chopsticks or your fingers to dip the slices in a little bowl of soy sauce or spicy mayo and eat them in one bite!

MAKES: 4 BOWLS OR 8 SUSHI ROLLS
SKILL LEVEL: 3 🍴🍴🍴
TOTAL TIME: 20 MINUTES (PLUS RICE COOKING TIME)

GF **NF**

NUTRITIONAL BENEFITS
Seaweed contains iodine. Iodine is a vital nutrient for our thyroid, which regulates our energy and body temperature and supports our growth and development.

Spicy Cashew Mayo

If you like spicy food, you'll love this with your sushi!

BLEND TOGETHER:

1/2 cup raw cashews (soaked for at least 10 minutes in hot water if you don't have a powerful blender)	1 TBSP lime juice
	2 tsp maple syrup
	2 tsp soy sauce
	1 TBSP sriracha sauce (use a little less at first and taste)
1/3 cup water	

Toaster Chips

Make chips by putting corn tortillas in a regular toaster like toast!

INGREDIENTS
Corn tortillas

INSTRUCTIONS

1. In a regular toaster, toast corn tortilla once on medium level. Flip over so the top goes to the bottom, and toast again until golden brown.

2. Let cool completely, then break into pieces.

(Instead of a toaster, you can bake chips in the oven at 400 degrees for 15–17 minutes until golden and crispy.)

CONFETTI BLACK BEAN SALSA WITH TOASTER CHIPS

Crunchy chips and colorful salsa make a yummy lunch, snack, or party food!

Ingredients

1 can black beans (or 1 1/4 cups, cooked)
1 bell pepper, chopped
1/2 cup chopped red onion
1 cup chopped tomatoes
1 (or 1/2, if preferred) jalapeño, seeds removed and minced (optional)
1/2 cup cilantro, chopped fine

1-2 avocados, chopped
1 1/2 cups corn (fresh or frozen)
2 TBSP red wine vinegar
2 TBSP lime juice
1 tsp salt
1 tsp cumin
Toaster Chips (see opposite)

Instructions

1 Drain and rinse the black beans.

2 Chop the bell pepper, onion, tomatoes, jalapeño (if using), cilantro, and avocados. If you're using a jalapeño, wear gloves while cutting it because the juice can make your hands burn for hours afterward.

3 Stir all the ingredients together, but add the avocado just

before serving to prevent it from getting brown. Taste and add a little more salt or cumin if you'd like.

4 Serve immediately with chips or keep in the fridge. Flavors get better if the salsa can sit for a few hours before eating it.

NUTRITIONAL BENEFITS
Beans and vegetables help prevent diabetes and cancer—two of the most common diseases in the U.S. They keep blood sugar stable for a long time and contain tons of tiny nutrients called phytochemicals that fight disease.

TIP
You can make this into a meal by using it as a taco filling. Put the salsa into corn tortillas and enjoy—they don't need anything else!

HOW TO PLAN AND PACK A HEALTHY LUNCH

You have a *lot* of lunches ahead of you in life! Every day as a child or adult, you'll need to figure out what to eat for lunch at school, home, or work. Here are some tips:

- **PICK OUT ONE OR TWO FRUITS OR VEGETABLES.** These foods have lots of fiber and water that fill you up, along with tons of tiny nutrients called *micronutrients* that can keep you healthy and prevent disease.
- **PICK A FOOD THAT HAS WHOLE GRAINS OR STARCHY VEGETABLES.** This can ensure you get enough calories (i.e., energy!). For example, a baked potato, roasted butternut squash, pasta, corn, quinoa, brown rice, whole-grain pancake, granola, tortilla, or the bread of a sandwich can all work.
- **ADD A NUT, SEED, BEAN, OR LENTIL.** These foods add even *more* micronutrients, along with protein, healthy fats, and fiber. You might choose peanut butter, hummus, tofu, lentils, kidney beans, edamame, peas, almonds, pistachios, pumpkin seeds, or even soy milk. Healthy treats often have these ingredients (like our Energy Balls on page 123 or Chocolate Chip {Chickpea} Cookie Bars on page 168!)

Eat a variety of foods, and you'll get a broad variety of nutrients to keep your body healthy.

QUICK IDEAS:

Need inspiration? Here are some super-easy meal combinations worth trying!

- Bean burrito + baby tomatoes + dried fruit
- Chickpea pasta with tomato sauce + grapes + peas
- Peanut butter banana sandwich + bell pepper sticks
- Veggie burger on bun + banana + pumpkin seeds
- Noodles with tofu, veggies, and soy sauce + orange
- Carrot sticks + Yummest Hummus (page 115) + pita bread
- Black bean soup + whole-grain crackers + mango
- Baked sweet potato + black beans + salsa + guacamole on top
- Broccoli + brown rice + tofu with salt and pepper
- Orange + mixed nuts + whole-grain muffin
- Pasta Salad (page 69) + Energy Balls (page 123)
- Chickpea Salad Sandwich (page 57) + cantaloupe
- Ants on a log + leftover Fluffy Pancakes (page 33)
- Baked oatmeal + apple slices + cucumber slices
- Nutty Noodles (page 81) + grapes

"Whoever said eating healthy isn't convenient has never eaten an apple!"

—Dr. Michael Greger in *How Not to Die*

TIP

Make large batches of muffins (like the Banana Mini Muffins on page 131), breakfast cookies (like the Carrot Cake Breakfast Cookies on page 29), burritos (like the Breakfast Burritos on page 31), pancakes (find a mix for Fluffy Pancakes on page 33), veggie burgers (like the Bravo Bean Burgers on page 83), or Energy Balls (see page 123) and keep some in the freezer so you have something you can quickly grab on a busy morning.

LUNCH

TIP

A simple way to pack a lunch is to set aside some of your dinner meal for lunch the next day.

WHOLE-FOOD, PLANT-BASED PACKAGED SNACKS

*H*ere are some fairly nutritious snacks you can buy that are ready to eat. They are perfect for traveling or busy days. Some of them are not 100% whole foods, but they are pretty close.

- Lära Bars
- That's It bars
- Fruit leather with no added sugars
- Brad's Kale Chips
- Raisin boxes
- Individual bags of baby carrots (sold in produce section)
- Individual hummus cups
- Skout Organics Bars
- Bob's Red Mill Oatmeal Cups
- Individual cups of olives
- Fruit cups in 100% juice (in canned fruit aisle)
- Small bags of nuts (like Wonderful Pistachios)

- KIND bars (these have 5 grams of added sugar)
- Go Raw brand sprouted snacking seeds
- Small packages of roasted seaweed
- Mary's Gone Crackers
- Rice cakes with no ingredients besides rice and salt
- Individual bags of Seapoint Farms dry roasted edamame
- Bare dried fruit chips (freeze-dried fruit)
- Guacamole cups
- Applesauce pouches

A GUIDE TO
EPIC VEGGIE SANDWICHES

*E*xperiment with sandwiches until you figure out what kinds are your favorite!

- **BASE**: whole-grain bread, tortilla, pita bread, or lettuce
- **SPREAD**: pesto, Yummest Hummus (see page 115), mashed avocado, mustard
- **FILLINGS**: sliced tomato, cucumber, lettuce, spinach, pickles, bell peppers, grated carrot, sauerkraut, red onion, sprouts, sliced apple, sliced baked tofu, or tempeh
- **FINISHING TOUCH**: sunflower or pumpkin seeds, salt and pepper, drizzle of salad dressing

SOME FAVORITE COMBOS:

- Bread + Yummest Hummus (see page 115) + spinach + olives (grilled on a skillet)
- Rice cake + avocado + tomato + mustard
- Pita bread + Yummest Hummus (see page 115) + tomato + cucumber + spinach + pesto or mustard
- Tortilla + refried beans + avocado + salsa + lettuce

DINNER

NUTTY NOODLES

MAKES: 4 SERVINGS
SKILL LEVEL: 3 ❘❘❘
TOTAL TIME: 25 MINUTES

GF

For gluten-free, use brown rice noodles.

Ingredients

1 package (8 oz) whole-wheat spaghetti noodles
1 batch of Peanut Sauce (see page 140)
1 cucumber, peeled and diced
1 bell pepper, chopped
1 carrot, grated or cut into thin sticks

3 green onions
1/2 bunch cilantro
Peanuts for garnish
Optional: lettuce leaves (to serve as lettuce wraps)

Instructions

1 Boil a pot of water and cook pasta according to directions. Drain in a colander.

2 Prepare Peanut Sauce (see page 140).

3 Cut vegetables. Slice green onions and chop cilantro.

4 Stir noodles, sauce, and vegetables together. Garnish with additional cilantro and peanuts.

5 Serve warm or cold. You can also eat it inside a piece of lettuce for a lettuce wrap.

QUICK MEAL

If you make extra patties, you can freeze the cooked burgers in an air-tight container. Warm them up in the microwave or air fryer for a quick meal.

BLENDING TIP

If you don't have a food processor, blend the oats and nuts together in a blender and stir with the rest of the ingredients. Mash the beans with a fork until smooth and stir everything together.

"MEAT"BALL ALTERNATIVE

Little ones might prefer these made into balls instead of burger patties. They can dip the balls into ketchup, etc.

TOPPING IDEAS

- Whole-grain buns (or pieces of lettuce for lettuce wrap)

- Ketchup, mustard, or BBQ sauce

- Yummest Hummus (see page 115)

- Guacamole (see page 62)

- Paprika Eureka Sauce (see page 136)

- Lettuce, tomato, pickles, thinly sliced pineapple, or sauerkraut

To serve gluten-free, use gluten-free buns or a piece of lettuce.

BRAVO BEAN BURGERS

These burgers are yummy and easy to make. They are not spicy. Bean burgers are best with lots of sauces and a really good bun. Your family will tell you "Bravo!" after they eat these, which means, "You did great!"

MAKES: 8 BURGERS
SKILL LEVEL: 2 🍴
TOTAL TIME: 40 MINUTES

GF

NF

For nut-free, use pumpkin or sunflower seeds instead of nuts.

Ingredients

- 2 (15-oz) cans black beans or kidney beans (or 3 cups cooked beans)
- 1 tsp onion powder
- 1 tsp garlic powder
- 1 cup rolled oats
- 1/2 cup walnuts, cashews, pecans, sunflower seeds, or pumpkin seeds
- 2 TBSP maple syrup
- 2 TBSP red wine vinegar
- 2 TBSP soy sauce
- 2 tsp chili powder

NUTRITIONAL BENEFITS
Beans keep your blood sugar stable, which gives you consistent energy.

Instructions

1. Preheat the oven to 350 degrees. Get out a baking sheet and line it with parchment paper or a silicone mat. Open the cans of beans and pour them into a colander in the sink and rinse well.

2. In a food processor, blend together all the ingredients except the beans until fine and the nuts, seeds, and oats are the size of coarse sand.

3. Add half the beans and run the food processor for several seconds until well combined. Add the rest of the beans and this time pulse the food processor, or stir the beans in by hand, so there is some variety in texture.

4. Use a 1/3 cup measure to scoop the mixture out onto the baking sheet. Shape the mixture into burger patty shapes.

5. Bake for 20 minutes. Flip the burgers and bake for 10 more minutes. Let them cool at least a little bit so they firm up more. While they bake and cool, prepare the toppings.

6. Serve on whole-grain buns or in a lettuce wrap with your favorite burger toppings.

Instant Pot Version

INSTRUCTIONS

1. Set the sauté setting for 5 minutes and sauté the onions, garlic, carrots, and bell pepper. Add a tablespoon of water if it starts to stick.

2. Add the broth, thyme, oregano, coconut milk, and potatoes and set on high pressure for 5 minutes.

3. Do either a quick or natural release, and then add frozen corn and more salt and pepper to taste.

4. To thicken it up a bit, mash a few of the potatoes with a fork against the side of the pot or use an immersion blender.

POTATO CORN CHOWDER

Ingredients

1 onion, diced

3 large garlic cloves, minced (or 2 tsp garlic powder)

3 large carrots, sliced thin

5 medium potatoes, diced

1 red bell pepper, diced

5 cups vegetable broth

1 tsp thyme

1 tsp oregano

1/2 tsp each salt and pepper

2 cups frozen corn

3/4 cup canned full-fat coconut milk
OR 1 can (13 oz) of light coconut milk

Instructions

1 Sauté the onion, garlic, and carrots in a small amount of water for about 5 minutes until fragrant.

2 Add potatoes, bell pepper, broth, and seasoning. Simmer over medium heat until potatoes and carrots are tender, about 15 minutes.

3 Add corn and coconut milk and let it heat through. Use a potato masher or a fork against the side of the pot to mash some of the potatoes to thicken the soup, or use an immersion blender.

COCONUT MILK ALTERNATIVE

If you don't like coconut milk, you can blend 3/4 cup cashews with 1 cup water until smooth and use that instead of the coconut milk. You can also use 1 1/2 cups soy milk instead of the coconut milk.

MASH 'EM!

Prefer mashed potatoes
instead of mouse potatoes?
Peel potatoes and cut
them into fourths. Boil
until tender. Drain, then
mash them with a fork
or potato masher with a
splash of plant milk, salt,
and pepper until they're
creamy and taste just
right. Serve with gravy. So
easy and satisfying!

MOUSE BAKED POTATOES WITH GRAVY

MAKES: 8 POTATOES
SKILL LEVEL: 3 🍴🍴🍴
TOTAL TIME: 25 MIN (AFTER BAKING POTATOES)

 GF

NUTRITIONAL BENEFITS

Potatoes are an excellent source of potassium, which is very good for your heart! A hundred thousand times a day, potassium plays a role in triggering your heart to squeeze blood through your body. Potassium is a mineral that is essential to health. Too little potassium is associated with heart disease, which is the number-one most common disease in America.[16]

Ingredients

8 oval Russet potatoes, baked (see page 111 for how to bake potatoes)

1 TBSP nutritional yeast (optional)

1/2 cup plant milk (soy is creamiest)

1/2 tsp salt

1/2 tsp pepper

1 tsp garlic powder

1 carrot

Some frozen peas

Uncooked spaghetti noodles

Instructions

1. Once the potatoes are baked and cool enough to handle, cut a football shape out of the top and carefully scoop out the potato with a spoon into a bowl. In a large bowl with a fork, mash the potato guts with nutritional yeast, milk, salt, pepper, and garlic powder.

2. Scoop the potato mixture back into the potato skins.

3. Decorate with carrot slice ears, pea eyes and nose, and noodle whiskers. Warm up in the oven or microwave, if desired. Serve with hot gravy (see page 138). Remove noodle whiskers before eating.

HAWAIIAN HAYSTACKS

For a nut-free sauce, use the gravy recipe on page 138.

Ingredients

1 cup brown rice, dry

TOPPINGS (CHOP EVERYTHING SMALL)
Green onions
Tomatoes
Peas
Bell pepper
Olives
Flaked coconut
Chopped peanuts, almonds, or cashews

Grated carrots
Mandarin oranges
Celery
Canned or fresh pineapple

SAUCE
1 cup raw cashews
3 cups vegetable broth
Salt and pepper

Instructions

1   Cook the rice and prepare your chosen toppings.

2   Make the gravy by blending the cashews and vegetable broth together in a high-speed blender until very smooth. Pour it into a pot and heat on medium heat until thick. Add salt and pepper to taste.

3   Let everyone assemble their haystacks with rice, sauce, and their favorite toppings.

EASY BREADSTICKS

Make simple "breadsticks"
to dip into your soup by
cutting whole-grain toast
into strips. Spray with
a little olive oil if you
like. Enjoy dipping them
into your soup!

ALPHABET SOUP

In Spanish, this is called "Sopa de letras." Have fun spelling with your dinner!
Make the Plant-Based "Parm" (see page 46) to sprinkle on top!

To make it gluten-free, use either Banza chickpea alphabet pasta or Probios brand of alphabet corn pasta. Alternatively, use diced potato or skip the pasta altogether for a yummy vegetable soup.

Ingredients

1 yellow onion, diced
4 cloves garlic, minced
6 cups vegetable broth
3 cups fresh or frozen vegetables, such as peas, corn, carrots, potatoes (or 1 16-oz bag frozen mixed vegetables)
1 can (6 oz) tomato paste
1 can (14 oz) petite diced tomatoes
1 cup dry alphabet pasta*

1 can (15 oz) white or kidney beans, drained (optional)
2 tsp Italian seasoning
1/2 tsp curry powder
1/2 tsp black pepper
1 tsp salt

*100% whole-grain alphabet pasta does not seem to exist, but you can order Eden Foods brand, which is 60% whole-grain. Regular alphabet pasta is found in most grocery stores in the Mexican food aisle.

Instructions

1. Dice and mince the onion and garlic. Measure the vegetable broth and have it nearby.

2. Put the onions and garlic in a large pot and turn onto medium-high heat. Sauté until the onions start to look translucent (see-through). When the bottom of the pot starts to turn brown, pour the vegetable broth in and stir to de-glaze the pan (that means liquid is added and the brown parts on the bottom come up).

3. Add the remaining ingredients and bring to a simmer (gentle boil). Let simmer for 10-15 minutes, or until the pasta and carrots are soft. Stir frequently, scraping the bottom, so the pasta doesn't stick.

4. Taste and add more salt and pepper if needed. If you like spicy food, add some red pepper flakes to your bowl.

TIP
Even if you don't usually like tahini, you can't taste it here and it makes a delicious stir-fry sauce. You can make the sauce ahead of time so prep is quick. Or, instead of making the sauce, just squirt some soy sauce on and call it good!

STIR-FRY

GF **NF**

Ingredients

2 cups cooked brown rice or rice noodles

4-6 cups chopped vegetables (such as broccoli, carrots, cauliflower, asparagus, peppers, snap peas, etc.; a 16-oz bag of frozen stir-fry vegetables works as well.)

1 block extra-firm tofu (optional)

1 TBSP soy sauce

Sesame seeds, as garnish

STIR-FRY SAUCE

2 cloves garlic

1 inch fresh ginger root

1/4 cup maple syrup (or frozen pineapple juice concentrate)

1/4 cup low-sodium soy sauce

2 TBSP lime juice or rice vinegar

1/3 cup tahini or peanut butter (omit for a non-creamy sauce)

1 TBSP cornstarch or arrowroot starch

2 TBSP water

Instructions

1 Cook rice or noodles, if you haven't already. Chop your chosen vegetables into small pieces.

2 Drain the tofu and cut it into cubes or tear it into pieces. Toss in a bowl with 1 TBSP soy sauce and let it marinate briefly. (If you'd like crispy tofu instead, prepare the Crispy Tofu on page 61.)

3 In a small blender, blend all the sauce ingredients together.

4 Heat up a large, nonstick skillet on medium-high heat (if you don't have nonstick, use a little oil). Cook the tofu until golden brown, about 5 minutes. Use a spatula to transfer it to a plate.

5 Put the vegetables into the hot, empty skillet with 1/4 cup water. Turn the heat to medium-high. Cover with a lid and stir occasionally until the vegetables are crisp-tender (that means not too soft and still with a little crunch) and all the water has cooked off.

6 Add the tofu back in. Pour the sauce over the stir-fry and stir until it is well-coated and the sauce has thickened. Serve with rice or noodles. Sprinkle with sesame seeds if you want to be fancy.

NUTRITIONAL BENEFITS

Broccoli and tofu have lots of calcium. Calcium is essential for bone and teeth growth, but also for allowing your muscles to contract, your heart to beat, and your blood to clot. Kids ages 1-3 need 700 mg of calcium a day, ages 4-8 need 1000 mg, and ages 9-13 need 1300 mg. One serving of firm tofu has about 250 mg of calcium. A cup of fortified soy milk has 300 mg of calcium (which is the same as cow milk). Those who drink dairy milk have higher rates of type 1 diabetes, cancer, and heart disease. So, it's best to get calcium from plant sources.[17]

PASTA ALFREDO

Cook pasta and veggies to go with this delicious sauce, and you have a fancy, very yummy meal!

Ingredients

1 1/2 cups diced onion
4 large garlic cloves, minced
1 cup cauliflower florets (fresh or frozen)
1 cup vegetable broth
1/2 cup water
1/2 cup raw cashews
1 TBSP lemon juice

1/4 tsp salt
1/4 tsp pepper
2 TBSP nutritional yeast
1 package (16 oz) whole-grain or legume pasta, such as spaghetti or linguine
Steamed vegetables to serve on the side

Instructions

1. Over medium heat, sauté the onion, garlic, and cauliflower in a skillet with the vegetable broth until the broth has evaporated away and the cauliflower is soft, about 8–10 minutes.

2. While the vegetables are cooking, put the water, cashews, lemon juice, salt, pepper, and nutritional yeast in a blender.

3. Add the cooked vegetables to the blender. Blend until very smooth.

   Add more nutritional yeast if you want a more cheesy flavor, and add more salt and pepper to taste.

4. Boil your favorite pasta according to package directions. Drain. Steam some vegetables to serve with the pasta.

5. Pour the alfredo sauce on top of the pasta and enjoy! The sauce keeps well in the fridge for about 3 days.

For cashew-free, you can use 1/2 cup almonds (soaked in hot water 20 minutes or overnight).

For nut-free, use 1/2 cup white beans, or an additional cup of cauliflower. The texture may not be as creamy, but will still be yummy!

For gluten-free, use gluten-free pasta such as brown-rice or chickpea pasta.

Instant Pot Version

INSTRUCTIONS

1. In the Instant Pot, combine the lentils, broth, and Taco Seasoning.

2. Set to high pressure for 15 minutes. Let it release naturally (don't flip the valve).

Easy Pico de Gallo

Make this simple fresh salsa to serve on tacos or any other Mexican dish.

INGREDIENTS

2 large tomatoes, finely chopped

1/4 cup red or white onion, finely chopped

1/4 cup cilantro leaves and stems, chopped

1 lime

Salt

INSTRUCTIONS

1. Stir tomatoes, onion, and cilantro together with the juice of a lime and a few dashes of salt.

LENTIL TACOS

MAKES: 8-10 TACOS
SKILL LEVEL: 2
TOTAL TIME: 30 MINUTES

GF NF

Ingredients

1 1/2 cups dry lentils
3 cups vegetable broth
2 TBSP Taco Seasoning (see page 20)
Corn or flour tortillas

TOPPINGS
Chopped lettuce
Guacamole (see page 62)
Chopped cilantro
Salsa
"Cheese" Sauce (see page 139)
Easy Pico de Gallo (see opposite)

Instructions

1. Bring the lentils, broth, and Taco Seasoning to a boil. Reduce the heat to low, cover, and let the lentils gently simmer for 20-30 minutes until tender. Set a timer so you don't let them burn.

2. While the lentils cook, prepare the toppings: wash and cut lettuce, make the guacamole, and chop cilantro.

3. Right before eating, warm the corn tortillas wrapped in a damp towel in the microwave for about 30 seconds.

4. Once the lentils are cool enough, assemble tacos with all your favorite toppings.

5. Keep leftover lentils in the fridge for up to 5 days, or freeze for up to 3 months, then let them thaw in the fridge or counter and reheat.

Easy Pico de Gallo

NUTRITIONAL BENEFITS

Lentils are nutritional powerhouses with lots of fiber, protein, B vitamins, and iron. They are very low in fat, and, like all plant foods, contain no cholesterol. They are not only good for your body, but for the planet! It takes 5 gallons of water to produce every 1 gram of protein in lentils, but 29 gallons of water to produce every gram of protein from beef.[19]

GET CREATIVE!

Mix in some "Cheese" Sauce (see page 139) or fill the tortillas with taco lentils (see page 97). Or, make Tater Taquitos by putting some mashed potatoes (see page 86) into the corn tortillas! These are called "Tacos Dorados de Papa" in Mexico.

TAQUITOS

MAKES: 12 TAQUITOS
SKILL LEVEL: 2
TOTAL TIME: 30 MINUTES

GF NF

Ingredients

FILLING

1 can (16 oz) fat-free refried beans
1 cup cooked rice
1 cup frozen corn
1 TBSP Taco Seasoning (see page 20)
1 TBSP lime juice
Salt to taste

TO SERVE

12 corn tortillas (the extra-thin
   variety seems to not crack as much)
Salsa and/or guacamole (see page
   62) for dipping

Instructions

1 Preheat oven to 400 degrees.

2 Mix the filling ingredients all together in a large bowl.

3 Get a clean dish towel and wet it under the kitchen faucet. Wring it out so it's damp. Wrap it around the stack of corn tortillas and microwave for 60 seconds, or until the tortillas are very warm and pliable. If they are cold, they will break.

4 Put a small scoop of filling (a little less than 1/4 cup) down the middle of each tortilla and roll them up. Set them seam-side down on a baking sheet.

5 Bake for 15-20 minutes, until golden brown and crispy. You can also air-fry them at 370 degrees for 10 minutes.

TIP
Unbaked taquitos freeze well! Complete steps 1 through 4, then put the baking sheet of unbaked taquitos in the freezer. Once they are frozen, transfer them to a zip-top bag and store in the freezer for up to 3 months. Bake from frozen (no need to thaw) for 15-20 minutes at 400 degrees until golden brown and crispy (or for 10 minutes in an air fryer at 370 degrees).

Instant Pot Version

INSTRUCTIONS

1. In the Instant Pot, whisk together the milk, only 2 cups of vegetable broth, tahini, garlic powder, onion powder, nutritional yeast, and rice. Add 1/2 tsp salt. Do not include cornstarch.

2. Set Instant Pot to high pressure for 20 minutes. Once done, do a quick or natural release (flip the valve, or not—your choice).

3. In a separate pot on the stove, steam the broccoli by putting the broccoli and about 1 inch of water in a pot with a lid. Set to medium-high heat. Once water starts to simmer, set timer for 5 minutes. Broccoli should be tender. Remove from heat and drain off water.

4. Stir the broccoli and chickpeas into the rice once it is done.

EASY "CHEESY" BROCCOLI RICE CASSEROLE

MAKES: 4-6 SERVINGS
SKILL LEVEL: 2
TOTAL TIME: 80 MINUTES
GF NF

Put this in the oven, and then it's hands-off for an hour until it's time to eat!

Ingredients

- 1 can chickpeas, drained (optional)
- 3-4 cups broccoli florets (about 1 pound)
- 1 cup uncooked long-grain brown rice
- 4 cups vegetable broth
- 1/2 cup plant milk
- 1/2 tsp turmeric
- 2 tsp garlic powder
- 2 tsp onion powder
- 1/4 cup nutritional yeast
- 2 TBSP cornstarch or arrowroot powder
- 2 TBSP tahini or sunflower seed butter

Instructions

1. Preheat oven to 400 degrees. Lay chickpeas and broccoli across the bottom of a 9x13-inch pan.

2. Sprinkle the uncooked rice over the top of the chickpeas and broccoli.

3. Put the broth, milk, spices, nutritional yeast, cornstarch, and tahini in a medium-size pot and whisk it together. Bring to a boil.

4. Pour boiling mixture over the rice. With a spoon, push any rice sticking out into the liquid. (Tell the rice it can't escape the boiling lava, sorry.)

5. Cover with foil and bake for 60 minutes. Let it cool for at least 10 minutes before eating, for the rice to further absorb the liquid.

6. When eating, add salt and pepper to taste.

NUTRITIONAL BENEFITS
It is recommended to aim for at least 1/2 cup of cruciferous vegetables a day, such as broccoli. This is because of their unique nutrients, especially sulforaphane, which is super good at boosting your immune system, improving gut health, and preventing cancer.[20]

Slow-Cooker Version

INSTRUCTIONS

1. In the slow-cooker, cover the bottom with marinara sauce.

2. Layer some uncooked lasagna noodles (break them to fit), 1/3 of the "ricotta" filling, and 1/3 of the veggies.

3. Repeat until all your ingredients are used up. Make noodles and sauce the top layer.

4. Cook on low for 3-4 hours, or until noodles are soft. Lasagna will be a little runnier and more watery than oven-cooked lasagna, but still delicious and convenient!

LAZY LASAGNA

This easy lasagna requires no chopping and no boiling of noodles! The homemade "ricotta" is delicious.

For gluten-free, use Barilla Gluten-Free Oven-Ready Lasagna noodles or Banza Chickpea Lasagna Noodles.

Ingredients

HOMEMADE "RICOTTA"
1 package (12-16 oz) extra-firm tofu
2 TBSP lemon juice or red wine vinegar
1 tsp Italian seasoning or dried basil
1 tsp garlic powder
1 tsp salt
1/4 cup nutritional yeast

LASAGNA
2 (24-oz) jars marinara sauce
1 package whole-wheat or gluten-free lasagna noodles (they do not necessarily need to say oven-ready)
Fresh spinach or frozen peas (optional)
Basil leaves, for garnish

Instructions

1. Make the "ricotta" first by crumbling the tofu into a food processor and adding the remaining "ricotta" ingredients. Process until it's smooth.

2. Preheat oven to 350 degrees. Get out a 9x13-inch pan.

3. Pour enough sauce to cover the bottom of the pan with about 1/2 inch. Lay 3-4 noodles across the sauce. Spread some "ricotta" onto each noodle, using about 1/3 of the ricotta for each layer of lasagna. Sprinkle on spinach or peas, if using. Then pour more sauce on top. Layer more noodles, ricotta, vegetables, and sauce until the ingredients are all used up. Pour sauce over the top as the last ingredient.

4. Cover with foil or an upside-down baking sheet (this is important so the moisture stays in and cooks the noodles). Bake for 1 hour. Remove the foil or baking sheet and let lasagna cool for at least 15 minutes to set up. Garnish with basil leaves (if you have some).

MAKE IT CREAMY WITH HUMMUS
Although it adds an ingredient, adding 1 cup of hummus to the "ricotta" is creamy and delicious.

Hominy is corn kernels that
have been treated to have
a chewy texture. It is so
yummy in this soup!

SOUP-ER SIMPLE
WHITE BEAN CHILI

MAKES: 4-6 SERVINGS
SKILL LEVEL: 2 🍴
TOTAL TIME: 15 MINUTES

Salsa verde is a green salsa that is usually not very spicy. Verde (ver-day) means "green" in Spanish. You can use any kind of white beans, such as cannellini, navy, Great Northern, or chickpeas. It's a great recipe to make when you are out of fresh groceries.

Ingredients

1 jar (16 oz) mild salsa verde
3 cups low-sodium vegetable broth
3 cans white beans, drained and rinsed
1 can hominy (15-25 oz), drained
   (or 1 1/2 cups frozen corn)
1 TBSP cumin
1 tsp garlic powder
1 tsp oregano
3/4 cup cashews
1 cup water

OPTIONAL TOPPINGS
Cilantro
Avocado
Lime wedges
Corn tortillas (or oil-free, baked
   corn tortillas, sold near tostada
   shells)
Salt and pepper
Hot sauce

Instructions

1. Combine all ingredients, except cashews and water, together in a pot and warm through on medium heat on the stove.

2. In a blender, blend the cashews and water until smooth. Stir into soup.

3. While the soup heats, prepare fresh ingredients if you'd like, such as cilantro, avocado, or lime wedges. Toast corn tortillas in the toaster until golden brown, being careful not to burn them (or your fingers!).

4. To serve, let everyone prepare their own bowl with broken tortilla chips and other toppings. Add salt and pepper if needed.

For nut-free, omit the cashew cream for a clear soup, or stir in a spoonful of tofu sour cream or vegan cream cheese. To make tofu sour cream, blend together 1 12-oz box of silken tofu with 1 TBSP cider vinegar and 1 TBSP lemon juice and about 1/4 tsp salt (more to taste).

MORE USES FOR TOFU CRUMBLES

There are lots of meals you can add the "Meaty" Tofu Crumbles to. Put them in chili, lasagna, tofu scramble, tacos, or even taco soup!

"MEATY" SPAGHETTI

GF NF

Ingredients

"MEATY" TOFU CRUMBLES
1 block (12 oz) extra-firm tofu
2 TBSP nutritional yeast
2 TBSP soy sauce

SPAGHETTI
1 box (16 oz) whole-wheat or legume
   spaghetti noodles
1 jar (32 oz) spaghetti sauce

Instructions

1. Preheat oven to 375 degrees. Get out a large baking sheet and line it with parchment paper or a silicone baking mat.

2. Stir the soy sauce and nutritional yeast together in a large bowl.

3. Open the tofu and drain the liquid into the sink. You don't need to press it, since all the liquid will bake out.

4. Crumble the tofu into the bowl with the soy sauce mixture. Toss it until well-coated. Spread the crumbles onto the baking sheet.

5. Bake for 35-45 minutes until golden brown and crispy.

6. While the crumbles are baking, boil water and cook the pasta according to the package directions. Stir the marinara sauce into the pasta, then the cooked crumbles.

7. Sprinkle with Plant-Based "Parm" (page 46) if you'd like. Serve with a green salad or steamed vegetables.

A GUIDE TO ROASTED VEGGIES AND FRIES

Roasting vegetables in the oven makes ordinary veggies taste amazing!

ROASTED VEGETABLES

Ingredients

Onion, bell peppers, mushrooms, zucchini, yellow squash, carrots, cauliflower, broccoli, Brussels sprouts, or potatoes

Olive or avocado oil (optional)

Salt

Other spices, such as onion or garlic powder or black pepper (optional)

Instructions

1 Preheat oven to 450 degrees.

2 Line baking sheet with parchment or a silicone baking mat or grease with a small amount of oil.

3 Chop veggies all about the same size, DO NOT MIX, and place on the pan in sections by type of veggie (this way if one type of veggie is done before another, you can easily take it off and cook the others a little longer).

4 Spray lightly with oil (optional) and sprinkle with a little salt and other spices if desired.

5 Bake, checking veggies after 25 minutes and removing any that are already tender and browned. Watch closely and roast for 20 minutes longer or until vegetables are well-cooked and browning on the edges.

TIPS

Ovens, pans, the type and size of veggie, and whether or not you use oil can all affect how long you need to roast your veggies. These simple tips should help:

- If your veggies are browning on the outside before they are fully cooked on the inside, lower the heat by about 50 degrees.
- If your veggies are cooked on the inside but still need to brown on the outside, use the broiler for a few minutes.
- If you have a convection setting on your oven, it will usually cook and brown the veggies more quickly and make them crispier.
- Veggies will roast better if they are not too crowded on the pan, so give them some space to breathe! Use multiple pans if needed.
- A silicone baking mat or parchment paper will prevent veggies from sticking to the pan without using oil. If you don't have these, spray or spread a little oil on the pan.

CLASSIC FRIES

Ingredients

Russet potatoes (about 1 large potato per person)

Bowl of ice water

Olive or avocado oil (optional)

Salt

Other spices such as onion or garlic powder, rosemary, or black pepper

Instructions

1. Preheat oven to 475 degrees and line a baking sheet with parchment paper or silicone baking mat.

2. Scrub the potatoes, peel if desired, then cut into shoestring fry shapes (about 1/4-inch thick). You can do this by cutting the potato lengthwise into slices that are 1/4-inch thick, then into 1/4-inch rows.

3. Put the potatoes into a large bowl of ice water. Let them soak for 10 minutes. This is the secret step that reduces the starch and helps them become nice and crispy!

4. Drain the potatoes well, spread onto a clean towel, and pat gently to dry. Then, spread them on a baking sheet.

5. If using oil, spray with a little oil. Sprinkle with salt and other spices if you want.

6. Bake for 20 minutes and check. If the potatoes seem to be getting crispy in one part of the pan and not another, stir and cook for 5-15 minutes longer until golden and crispy. Use the broiler for the last 2-3 minutes if you'd like them crispier, being careful to check often so they don't burn. Enjoy them fresh and warm from the oven.

SWEET POTATO FRIES

Ingredients

2 large sweet potatoes
Olive or avocado oil
  (optional)
Salt

Other spices such as onion
  or garlic powder or black
  pepper (optional)

Instructions

1. Preheat oven to 400 degrees.

2. Peel the sweet potatoes and cut them into fry shapes that are 1/4-1/2 inch thick. Do not cut them bigger than this, or they will not cook through.

3. Put them in a large bowl and toss with about 1 TBSP of olive or avocado oil (if you use oil). Sprinkle them with salt and pepper. You can also sprinkle with garlic powder, onion powder, cajun seasoning, Taco Seasoning (see page 20), or any other spices you like!

4. Line your baking sheet with parchment or a silicone mat. Spread the potatoes on the baking sheet so there is space between each slice (use two baking sheets if you're making a lot). Bake for 25-30 minutes, or until they are tender when pierced with a fork. If using two baking sheets, switch them at 15 minutes and bake about 15 minutes more. Next, turn the broil on and bake for 3-5 more minutes. Check carefully to make sure they don't burn. Remove from the oven when they are golden brown.

HOW TO COOK BASIC INGREDIENTS

Cooking beans and grains from scratch is cheaper than buying them canned and precooked, and it's easy once you learn how! Make big batches of cooked grains, beans, and lentils to use throughout the week. If you have an electric pressure cooker (such as an Instant Pot), use it! It usually cooks faster and turns off by itself to prevent burning. Freeze extra portions in zip-top bags or containers to thaw out later for quick meals.

HOW TO COOK RICE   1 cup dry rice = 2 cups cooked

 IN A PRESSURE COOKER: Put 1 cup dry brown rice and 1 1/2 cups cold water into the pressure cooker pot. Turn the valve to the sealed position. Set to high pressure for 20 minutes. Let it naturally release for at least 10 minutes before turning the valve to release the steam.

 ON THE STOVE: Put 1 cup dry brown rice and 2 cups water into a pot. Bring it to a boil, turn the heat to low, and let it simmer with the lid on. Set the timer for 45 minutes. It is done when the rice is tender and all the water has been absorbed.

HOW TO COOK LENTILS   1 cup dry lentils = 2 1/2 cups cooked

 IN PRESSURE COOKER: Put 1 cup dry brown or green lentils and 1 3/4 cups water or vegetable broth into the pressure cooker pot. Turn the valve to sealed position. Set to high pressure for 10 minutes, then let it naturally release for at least 10 minutes before turning the valve to release the steam. This method is not ideal for red or yellow lentils, since they cook quickly and get mushy when pressure cooked.

 ON STOVE: Into a pot, pour 3 cups water or vegetable broth and 1 cup dry lentils. Turn it to high heat and let it come to a boil. Reduce the heat to low and put a lid on the pot. Set the timer according to the list below. Test to see if the lentils are tender by spooning a few out and tasting them after they cool. Once done, take them off the heat and drain any excess water. If your lentils are still hard after cooking, they may be too old.

- Red or yellow lentils: 15-20 minutes
- Black lentils: 25 minutes
- Brown or green lentils: 25-35 minutes

HOW TO COOK QUINOA   1 cup dry quinoa = 3 cups cooked

 IN PRESSURE COOKER: Put in 1 cup dry quinoa and 2 cups water. Set to 1 minute high pressure, then let natural release for 10 minutes before flipping the valve to let the steam out.

ON THE STOVE: Put 1 cup dry quinoa and 2 cups water into a pot. Bring to a boil, then turn heat to low, cover pot with a lid, and set the timer for 15 minutes. When timer beeps, take quinoa off of heat and let it sit, covered, until you're ready to use it.

HOW TO COOK BEANS

Beans require soaking before cooking, unless you use a pressure cooker (like an Instant Pot). Even when using a pressure cooker, try to soak beans first to provide the best nutrition and texture. To do so, fill a large mixing bowl halfway with dry beans. Cover with water and let them sit overnight (or for at least 8 hours).

 IN PRESSURE COOKER: Pour out soaking water, rinse beans, and put soaked beans in the pressure cooker. Cover with water up to the maximum fill line. Add 2 tsp salt. Turn valve to sealed position. Set to high pressure for 20 minutes. If they are not soaked first, cook for 25-30 minutes (depending on how soft you want them). You can do a quick or natural release (turn the steam valve, or not).

 ON STOVE: Drain off soaking water, rinse beans, and put the soaked beans into a large pot. Cover with 2 inches of water and add 2 tsp salt. Bring the water to a boil, then reduce heat to low and let simmer, stirring occasionally, for 60 to 90 minutes.

HOW TO STEAM POTATOES

 IN A PRESSURE COOKER: Wash as many potatoes as you need. Put them in the pressure cooker with 1 inch of water. Turn valve to sealed position. Set to high pressure for 12 minutes, and do a quick release. Keep cooked potatoes in the fridge to eat as snacks with salt and pepper, to grate onto a skillet for hash browns, or to mash with plant milk and salt and eat with gravy.

HOW TO BAKE POTATOES

First, scrub the potatoes very well. Pierce each one with a fork a few times. Then, cook as follows:

 SLOW COOKER: Set potatoes in a crockpot and cook on high for about 2 hours, or on low 3-4 hours.

 OVEN: Bake at 400 degrees on the oven rack for about 60 minutes, until soft when you squeeze them with an oven mitt.

 MICROWAVE: Cook 4 potatoes at a time for 10-15 minutes. Wrap them in a towel and let them sit for about 15 more minutes to let the heat distribute evenly and finish cooking.

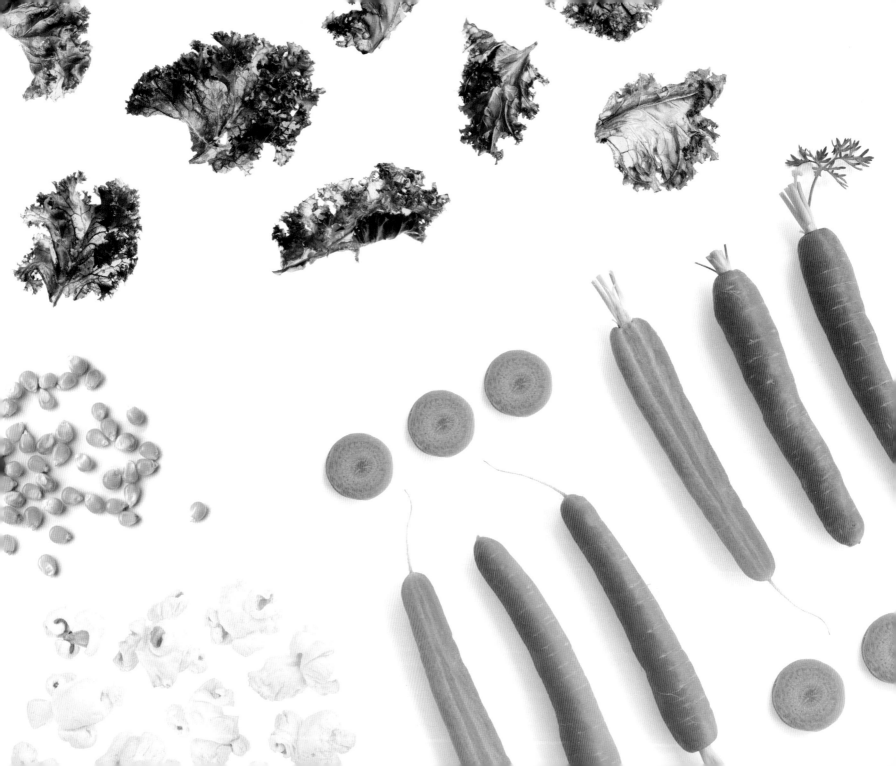

SIDES & SAUCES

Variations

RED PEPPER HUMMUS

Add 1 cup roasted red pepper when you add the chickpeas. You can buy roasted red peppers in a jar or roast them yourself and peel the skins off.

CURRY HUMMUS

Add 1 1/2 tsp curry powder and 1/2 of a diced jalapeño pepper (optional).

BEET HUMMUS

Boil a beet for about 20 minutes or until soft (or use canned ones that are not pickled). Peel, chop, and blend about 1 cup of beet pieces into the hummus. It makes a bright color and tastes delicious!

Red Pepper Hummus

THE YUMMEST
HUMMUS

MAKES: 2 CUPS
SKILL LEVEL: 2
TOTAL TIME: 15 MINUTES

GF **NF**

Chocolate Hummus

Ingredients

1 large clove garlic, chopped
1/4 cup lemon juice
1/4 cup cold water
1/2 cup tahini

1 can chickpeas, drained (or 1 1/2 cups cooked chickpeas)
1/2 tsp salt
1/2 tsp cumin

Instructions

1 Add the chopped garlic and lemon juice to the bowl of a food processor. Let it sit for about 10 minutes so the raw garlic loses its sharp flavor.

2 Add the water and tahini and process together.

3 Add the chickpeas, salt, and cumin and process until smooth. Taste and increase salt and spices to taste.

Curry Hummus

Beet Hummus

CHOCOLATE HUMMUS

1 can garbanzo beans or black beans, drained
1/4 cup peanut butter (or almond butter or tahini)

1/4 tsp salt
1/3 cup maple syrup (or 1/2 cup soft dates)
1/4 cup cocoa powder
1 tsp vanilla

1. Blend together until smooth. Serve with sliced bananas or apples, strawberries, pretzels, crackers, or pita bread.

TIP

If you're struggling to give up butter, try Miyoko's Creamery butter. It's not oil-free, but it's the yummiest plant-based butter we know of and has more whole ingredients than most. You can find it near the tofu and vegan products in most grocery stores.

CORNBREAD

Ingredients

DRY INGREDIENTS

2 cups cornmeal

1 cup whole wheat or spelt flour

1 1/2 cups almond flour

2 tsp salt

2 TBSP baking powder

WET INGREDIENTS

3/4 cup applesauce

1/4 cup maple syrup

2 1/2 cups plant milk

Instructions

1. Preheat oven to 400 degrees. Mix dry ingredients in a large bowl.

2. Make a well in the center and add wet ingredients. Mix well, but do not over-stir, as that creates tougher bread.

3. Pour into a greased 9x13-inch pan. For muffins, divide into a 12-cup muffin pan.

4. Bake for 25-30 minutes, or until golden and cracked on top and a toothpick comes out clean. Bake full-size muffins for 20-25 minutes.

For gluten-free, use 1 cup additional cornmeal to replace the whole wheat flour. Ensure your cornmeal is certified gluten-free, too. Bake for 40 minutes, or until firm to the touch. You can also use 1 cup gluten-free all-purpose flour instead of the whole wheat, but you will need to let the cornbread set for several hours after baking so the flour can fully absorb the moisture.

For low-fat or nut-free, leave the almond flour out and use 1/2 cup more cornmeal and 1 cup more flour.

TIP

For more tender biscuits,
use full-fat coconut milk
as your plant milk in the
recipe.

DROP BISCUITS

Tender biscuits usually have butter in them, but this recipe uses almond flour (or coconut milk) for a whole-food source of fat. They are easy to make and absolutely delicious with soup.

Ingredients

1 tablespoon apple cider vinegar

1 cup plant milk

DRY INGREDIENTS

1 1/2 cups whole wheat flour (use half white flour for more traditional biscuits)

1/2 cup almond flour

1 tablespoon baking powder

1/4 tsp baking soda

3/4 tsp salt

Instructions

1. Mix the vinegar with the plant milk in a liquid measuring cup and let it sit for 5 minutes. This curdles it like buttermilk.

2. Preheat oven to 450 degrees.

3. Mix the dry ingredients together.

4. Add the curdled milk and mix the dough together. Do not overmix, as that creates tough biscuits.

5. Line a baking sheet with parchment paper and drop large spoonfuls of dough to create 10 biscuits. Flatten them slightly into a circle.

6. Bake for 10-12 minutes or until lightly browned.

TIP

If you don't have apple cider vinegar, you can replace it with lemon juice to create the "buttermilk."

For nut-free, replace the almond flour with 1/2 cup more whole wheat or gluten-free flour and use 1 cup of full-fat coconut milk for the plant milk (try to use only the thick, creamy part at the top of the can).

For gluten-free, replace whole wheat flour with all-purpose gluten-free flour and use full-fat coconut milk for the plant milk.

A GUIDE TO SALADS

It's a great habit to eat some salad every day! It's a colorful way to get lots of nutrition and variety. Here's a foolproof way to make a tasty salad:

A PICK A BASE OR TWO

- Lettuce
- Chopped kale or cabbage (sprinkle with salt and massage so it's not so tough to chew)
- Spring mix
- Cooked pasta, rice, quinoa, or other grain

B CHOOSE FRUITS AND VEGGIES TO ADD

- Tomatoes
- Cucumbers
- Bell peppers
- Carrots
- Corn
- Peas
- Beets
- Apples
- Peaches
- Berries
- Avocado
- Roasted vegetables, such as sweet potatoes (see page 108)

C ADD SOME PLANT PROTEINS

- Crispy tofu
- Black beans
- Cooked rice, farro, quinoa, or other grain
- Kidney beans
- Chickpeas
- Lentils
- Slivered almonds
- Chopped walnuts
- Chopped pecans
- Pumpkin seeds
- Sunflower seeds
- Hemp seeds

D CHOOSE A DRESSING

- Hummus (see page 115) thinned out with water
- Guacamole (see page 62) thinned out with water
- Salsa
- Lemon juice
- Any of the dressings on pages 141–142

Variations

PUMPKIN ENERGY BALLS

Add 1/4 cup pumpkin purée, 1 tsp Pumpkin Spice Blend (see page 126), and 1/2 cup extra oats. Use pumpkin seeds instead of hemp seeds. Process in a food processor.

CHOCOLATE PEPPERMINT BALLS

Use almond butter and not peanut butter. Add 2 TBSP cocoa powder, 1/2 tsp peppermint extract, and chocolate chips. Process all together in a food processor until smooth.

Chocolate Peppermint Balls

TIP

If you'd like to use dates instead of maple syrup, put 2/3 cup packed soft dates in a food processor with all the remaining ingredients and run it until smooth.

ENERGY BALLS

You'll be a ball of energy after eating a couple of these! Make them for picnics, hikes, sports games, road-trip snacks, to give away, or for dessert!

MAKES: 24 BALLS
SKILL LEVEL: 1
TOTAL TIME: 15 MINUTES

GF

NF

Ingredients

1/2 cup peanut or almond butter

1/3 cup maple syrup

1/2 cup raisins or mini chocolate chips

1 cup rolled oats

1/4 cup ground flax seeds

1/4 cup hemp seeds

For nut-free, use sunflower seed butter or any other seed butter. As another option, use 1/2 cup cooked chickpeas blended until smooth instead of nut or seed butter.

Instructions

1 In a large bowl, mix together the peanut butter and maple syrup with a spoon. If you need to, warm it up in the microwave for 30 seconds to make stirring it easier.

2 Add the rest of the ingredients and stir well.

3 Roll into balls and enjoy!

Pumpkin Energy Balls

TIP
If energy balls are too sticky, roll in coconut, hemp seeds, or oat flour.

NUTRITIONAL BENEFITS
Spinach contains nitrates, which improve athletic performance and may bolster your muscle strength![21]

SHAMROCK
SHAKES

You know what's luckier than finding a four-leaf clover? Making mint chocolate chip milkshakes that are super yummy *and* healthy!

Ingredients

2 dates
3/4 cup plant milk
1 small handful of spinach
1-2 frozen bananas (about 2 cups frozen banana chunks)

2 TBSP dairy-free dark chocolate chips
1 drop peppermint essential oil or 1/2 tsp peppermint extract

Instructions

1. In a blender, blend the dates, milk, and spinach so the dates and spinach get well-combined.

2. Add the bananas, chocolate chips, and peppermint and blend until smooth.

TIP
For a fun treat, shakes can be frozen into mint chip popsicles instead!

Pumpkin Spice Blend

INGREDIENTS

3 TBSP ground
cinnamon

2 tsp ground
ginger

2 tsp ground
nutmeg

1 tsp ground
allspice

1 1/2 tsp
ground
cloves

INSTRUCTIONS

1. Mix together and keep in a jar. Make sure to label it!

PUMPKIN PEANUT BUTTER DIP WITH APPLES

MAKES: 1 CUP OF DIP
SKILL LEVEL: 1
TOTAL TIME: 15 MINUTES

GF

Ingredients

DIP
1/2 cup natural peanut butter
1/2 cup canned pumpkin purée
1 tsp Pumpkin Spice Blend (see opposite)
1/2 tsp cinnamon
1 tsp vanilla extract

1/4 cup maple syrup

FOR SERVING
Sliced apples
Chopped pecans (optional)
Cinnamon (optional)

Instructions

1. In a bowl, stir together all the ingredients. If you're making a large batch, mixing with an electric mixer is handy. Add more sweetener and Pumpkin Spice Blend to your liking, if needed.

2. Garnish with chopped pecans and extra cinnamon, if desired. Serve with sliced apples.

3. Keeps well in the fridge for 1 week in an airtight container.

TIP
This is also delicious with celery, bananas, or on toast or pumpkin pancakes.

MAKES: 5-10 SERVINGS

SKILL LEVEL: 3 🍴🍴🍴

TOTAL TIME: 1 HOUR 45 MINUTES

Easy 100% Whole Wheat Bread

3 cups whole wheat flour

1-2 cups additional whole wheat flour

1 1/2 tsp salt

1 TBSP yeast

1/4 cup vital wheat gluten

1/4 cup maple syrup

1 3/4 cups warm water (not hot, as that would kill the yeast)

1. Mix the 3 cups of flour, yeast, salt, and vital wheat gluten together with a whisk in a large bowl.

2. Mix honey and warm water together in a liquid measuring cup, then add to the dry ingredients until mixed well.

3. Let sit for 20-30 minutes to let the flour absorb some of the water.

4. Next, add 1 cup of additional flour, and up to an additional cup of flour (1/4 cup at a time, up to 5 cups total) until the dough is firm and sticky. I find 1 or 1 1/4 cups of flour is perfect. You want it sticky and not too stiff and dry, but still able to hold its shape and not be batter-like.

5. Knead for 10 minutes either by hand or with a stand mixer with a dough hook. The dough should be stretchy.

6. Cover the bowl with a towel and put it in a warm place. Let it rise for 45 minutes, or until doubled in size. On the counter is fine, or if your house is cold, put the bowl in the cold oven with the oven light on.

7. After rising, shape the bunny by continuing with step 2 on the opposite page. (Or, for a simple loaf of bread, put it in a loaf pan, let it rise again until double in size, and bake at 350 for 35-40 minutes).

BREAD BUNNY VEGGIE TRAY

My mom clipped this idea from a magazine in 1994, and I've been making
this wholesome hare since I was a kid! Let's hop to it!

Ingredients

1 loaf of your favorite whole-grain (or gluten-free) bread
  dough (you can use the recipe on the opposite page, or
  even buy Rhodes 100% Whole Wheat Frozen Bread Dough,
  which is vegan but does contain oil and sugar)

2 raisins

2 sliced almonds

2 TBSP plant milk mixed with 1 tsp maple syrup (creates an
  "egg wash" that makes the bread golden and shiny)

Raw vegetables, lettuce, and your favorite dip or hummus

Instructions

1. Line a baking sheet with parchment paper or a silicone baking mat.

2. Divide the loaf of dough in half. Cut one half into 1/4 and 3/4 portions. Shape the 3/4 portion into an egg shape for the body. Place it on a baking sheet.

3. Shape the 1/4 portion into a pear shape and set it above the body for the head. Pinch the dough together at the neck. Using clean scissors, clip two times on each side to form whiskers.

4. Take the other half of the loaf and cut it into four even quarters. Form two quarters into two ears by rolling each piece into a long rope, about 16 inches long. Fold each one together and place at the top of the head. Pinch the top ends of the ears to form a point.

5. With one of the remaining two quarters, make feet by dividing the dough in half and patting into two oval shapes. Clip toes using scissors.

6. Divide the last piece into 1/3 and 2/3 portions. Divide the 2/3 into two hands and place on the sides of the body. Clip fingers using scissors.

7. Divide the remaining 1/3 dough into two large balls for cheeks and one small ball for the nose. Place them on the bunny's face. Place two raisins for eyes and almonds for teeth.

8. Using a pastry brush or your fingers, brush everything with the "egg wash," even the teeth. Cover with a large plastic bag or a damp dish towel. Let it rise for 1 hour until it looks doubled in size. Remove the cover and bake at 350 degrees for 25-30 minutes until golden brown.

9. Let cool completely. Then, hollow out the tummy and line it with lettuce. Fill it up with hummus or dip. Surround the bunny with sliced vegetables.

Variations

BERRY-BANANA MUFFINS
Stir in 1/2 cup frozen blueberries, raspberries, or chopped strawberries to the batter.

PEANUT BUTTER BANANA MUFFINS
Add 1/3 cup peanut butter to the blender with the bananas.

CHOCOLATE BANANA MUFFINS
Leave out nutmeg and cinnamon. Add 1/3 cup cocoa powder and 1/4 cup more maple syrup or dates.

CUPCAKES
Frost with Healthy Chocolate Frosting (see page 164) to make these into dessert!

BANANA BREAD
Pour batter into a parchment-lined bread pan. Bake 50-60 minutes, or until a knife comes out clean.

BANANA MINI MUFFINS

Banana muffins are a yummy breakfast, snack, or treat! Add **1/4 cup** more dates or maple syrup if you want them sweeter.

MAKES: 24 MINI MUFFINS (OR 12 REGULAR MUFFINS)
SKILL LEVEL: 2 ▐▐
TOTAL TIME: 45 MINUTES

For nut-free, leave walnuts out.

For gluten-free, use 3 cups certified gluten-free oat flour instead of 2 1/2 cups whole wheat flour.

Ingredients

DRY INGREDIENTS
2 1/2 cups whole wheat flour
1 tsp cinnamon
1/2 tsp ground nutmeg
1 tsp baking powder
1/2 tsp baking soda
1/2 tsp salt

WET INGREDIENTS
3 medium overripe bananas
  (or 1 3/4 cup mashed)
1/2 cup dates (or 1/4 cup maple syrup)
1 cup plant milk
2 TBSP ground flax seeds

OPTIONAL MIX-INS
1/4 cup non-dairy chocolate chips
1/4 cup chopped walnuts

Instructions

1 Preheat the oven to 350 degrees. Grease a muffin pan or mini-muffin pan, or use a silicone pan instead.

2 Mix the dry ingredients in a large mixing bowl.

3 In a blender, blend the bananas, milk, dates (or maple syrup), and flax seeds together until smooth.

4 Pour the wet ingredients into the bowl of dry ingredients and stir until just combined (it will be too thick to mix all together in the blender, so use a bowl). Add the chocolate chips or nuts, if you are using them.

5 Use a cookie scoop or two spoons to fill muffin cups 3/4 full. Bake mini muffins for 17-20 minutes and large muffins for 22-25 minutes. Let cool completely. These muffins freeze well in a zip-top bag.

TIP
When you have ripe bananas, peel them, cut into chunks, and freeze in a bag. Thaw some out in the microwave and mash them when you want to make these muffins.

TIPS FOR YOUR CHARCUTERIE BOARD

- Use a cutting board, cookie sheet, big platter, or large plate.

- Have an odd number of small bowls. Put them on the board first to add structure.

- Arrange food in and around the bowls or in piles. Fill in empty places with nuts or dried fruit.

- Add some fresh herbs to make it pretty, like cilantro, parsley, thyme, or rosemary.

- The more variety, the better! Have a combination of sweet and savory.

CHARCUTERIE BOARDS

MAKES: AS MUCH AS YOU WANT!
SKILL LEVEL: 1
TOTAL TIME: 5-20 MINUTES

  Depending on your selections

Charcuterie (*shar-cute-er-ee*) boards are a beautiful display of food that you can eat with your fingers. You can pull out a bunch of different fruits, vegetables, nuts, seeds, and snacks you might already have on hand and put them together for a fun snack to enjoy with friends or family. To make it a meal, include ingredients to make little finger sandwiches, like bread and mustard.

Ideas

SAVORY

Jicama sticks

Avocado

Cherry tomatoes

Carrots

Cucumbers

Bell peppers

Celery

Any nuts or seeds

Roasted chickpeas

Edamame

Crispy Tofu (see page 61)

Olives

Pickles

Whole-grain crackers (Mary's Gone Crackers is an oil-free brand)

Whole-wheat pita bread cut into triangles

Rice cakes

Peanut butter

Hummus (see page 115)

Ranch Dip (see page 137)

Mini avocado toast

SWEET

Berries

Sliced apples

Orange slices

Grapes

Bananas

Pears

Dried fruit, such as raisins, apricots, mangoes, or figs

Energy Balls (see page 123)

Mini muffins

Chocolate Hummus (see page 115)

KALE CHIPS

Kale is one of the foods with the most nutrients per calorie. It is very powerful at preventing disease. And, these chips make it delicious and easy to eat lots of it!

Ingredients

1 large bunch kale
1 TBSP tahini
1 TBSP warm water
1 TBSP nutritional yeast
2 tsp lemon juice (or apple cider vinegar)

1/2 tsp paprika
1/2 tsp garlic powder
1/2 tsp salt (or a little less if you prefer)

Instructions

1. Preheat oven to 300 degrees or get out your air fryer.

2. Wash the kale and slide your fingers down the stem to remove the leaves. Tear the leaves into small pieces for chips, each about 3 inches square.

3. Mix the remaining ingredients in a large bowl. Toss the kale in it to coat the leaves. It's best to get your hands messy and massage the mixture into the kale.

4. Place on a baking sheet (or prepare to put the kale into an air fryer). Sprinkle with a little extra nutritional yeast.

5. Bake for 20 minutes, checking to see if they are crispy. If not, bake another 5-10 minutes. Or, air-fry in a single layer at a time at 370 degrees for about 4 minutes.

6. Enjoy within a day.

NUTRITIONAL BENEFITS
Kale provides sulphur-containing compounds called glucosinolates that make it taste bitter, but also make kale a very powerful cancer-fighting food. You can reduce the bitterness by massaging kale leaves until they are wilty and soft.[22]

GF

NF

For nut-free, you can use 2/3 cup vegan mayonnaise or 2/3 cup raw sunflower seeds instead of the cashews.

PAPRIKA EUREKA SAUCE

This is a delicious dip for eating roasted vegetables or fries, spreading on sandwiches, or slathering onto the Breakfast Burrito (see page 31) or Bravo Bean Burgers (see page 83).

Ingredients

2/3 cup raw cashews
1/3 cup water
3 TBSP lemon juice
2 tsp garlic powder (or 1 clove garlic)

1/2 tsp smoked paprika (add 1/2 tsp more if you like it really smoky)
1/2 tsp salt
Chipotle chili powder (optional for a spicy sauce)

Instructions

1 Soak the cashews in hot water for at least 20 minutes. Drain them.

2 Blend cashews with 1/3 cup water, lemon juice, and all the other ingredients together in a small blender.

3 Add a dash of chipotle chili powder if you like spicy sauces.

DID YOU KNOW?
Paprika is made of ground peppers, but not spicy ones (except hot paprika). Smoked paprika is a great way to add smoky flavors in plant-based cooking. Regular paprika (also called sweet paprika) does not have the smoked flavor.

136

RANCH DIP

Try to prioritize using fresh herbs for a very dill-icious dip or salad dressing! It's also yummy on bagels or veggie sandwiches.

Ingredients

2/3 cup raw cashews or raw sunflower seeds

3 TBSP lemon juice (about the juice of 2 lemons)

2/3 cup unsweetened plant milk (use 1 cup for thinner dressing)

2 tsp Dijon mustard

2 tsp garlic powder

1 tsp onion powder

1 tsp salt

1/2 tsp pepper

HERBS

1/4 cup fresh dill (or 1 tsp dried)

1/4 cup fresh parsley (or 1/2 tsp dried)

1/4 cup fresh chives (or 1 tsp dried)

Instructions

1. Soak cashews or sunflower seeds in hot water for 10 minutes. While they soak, pour the lemon juice and plant milk into a blender. This curdles and creates "buttermilk."

2. Drain cashews or sunflower seeds. Add them to the "buttermilk" in the blender, along with all other ingredients (except fresh herbs), and blend until smooth. Pulse in the fresh herbs (that means blend for just a second or two at a time).

3. Store in an airtight container in the fridge (for up to 5 days), and it will thicken. Serve as a dip for veggies, or spread on bagels or sandwiches like cream cheese.

MAKES: ABOUT 1 CUP

SKILL LEVEL: 2 🥄🥄

TOTAL TIME: 15 MINUTES

GF NF For nut-free, use the sunflower seeds instead of the cashews.

MAKES: 3 CUPS
SKILL LEVEL: 2
TOTAL TIME: 10 MINUTES

TIP
If you'd like to
make a mix for quick
gravy-making in
the future, combine
the dry ingredients
together and store
in a container with
written directions
to add the wet
ingredients and heat
until thick.

GRAVY

Ingredients

1/4 cup flour (either whole wheat or
   gluten-free all-purpose)
1 tsp onion powder
1/4 tsp black pepper
2 TBSP nutritional yeast

2 TBSP soy sauce
2 cups vegetable broth
1 cup unsweetened plant milk
1/2 tsp Italian seasoning (optional)

Instructions

1 Whisk all ingredients together
in a pot and cook over medium-
high heat until thick. Whisk

frequently to prevent lumps and
burning.

"CHEESE" SAUCE

Ingredients

- 2 cups water
- 1 large carrot, sliced
- 2 medium Yukon Gold potatoes, chopped
- 1/4 of a large onion
- 1/2 cup raw cashews
- 1 tsp garlic powder
- 1 tsp onion powder
- 1 tsp salt
- 1 TBSP apple cider vinegar (or lemon juice)
- 1/4 cup nutritional yeast

MAKES: 2 CUPS
SKILL LEVEL: 3
TOTAL TIME: 20 MINUTES

GF

Instructions

1. Boil 2 cups water in a small pot with a lid. Add the carrot, potatoes, onion, and cashews. Cover and cook 10 minutes, until potatoes and carrots are soft when pierced with a fork. Do not drain.

2. While it cooks, put the garlic powder, onion powder, salt, vinegar, and nutritional yeast into a blender.

3. Pour the cooked vegetables with the water into the blender and blend until smooth.

4. Pour onto pasta, baked potatoes, broccoli, or anything you like! Add salt and pepper on top to taste.

 QUICK VERSION

For a quick, nut-free "cheese" sauce, try this! In a pot, whisk the following together and heat on the stove until thick.

- 1 can (14 oz) coconut milk
- 1/4 cup tapioca starch
- 6 TBSP nutritional yeast
- 1 tsp onion powder
- 1 tsp salt

TIPS

- Use 2 cups of cauliflower florets instead of potatoes if you like.

- If you don't have Yukon Gold potatoes, you can use any other potato. Just peel them first.

- If you like spicy cheese sauce, stir in 1 small can of green chilies or 1 TBSP canned jalapeños.

- If you can't find (or don't like) nutritional yeast, you can leave it out. The sauce won't have as much flavor, but it's still tasty.

PEANUT SAUCE

You can use almond butter instead of peanut butter; it's yummy, too!

Ingredients

1/2 cup peanut butter
1/4 cup hot water
2 TBSP maple syrup
2 TBSP soy sauce
2 TBSP lime juice or vinegar
1/2 tsp garlic powder (or 1 tsp fresh minced garlic)

1/2 tsp ground ginger (or 1 tsp fresh grated ginger)
Dash of cayenne pepper or 1 tsp chili garlic sauce (optional)
1 TBSP sesame oil (optional)

Instructions

1. Stir all together in a bowl or blend in a small blender. Add 2 TBSP more water to make it thinner.

2. Serve on green salads, as a dip for raw veggies, or on noodles (such as the Nutty Noodles on page 81).

MAKES: 2/3 CUP
SKILL LEVEL: 1
TOTAL TIME: 15 MINUTES

GF

QUICK MEAL IDEA: PEANUT RICE & TOFU LETTUCE WRAPS
Crumble one package of extra-firm tofu into a skillet. Cook and stir until golden brown. Add 2 cups of cooked brown rice and stir in 1 batch of this peanut sauce. Serve in pieces of lettuce for lettuce wraps. Add cilantro, chopped peanuts, hot sauce, or the Spicy Cashew Mayo from page 71 if you'd like.

MAPLE BALSAMIC
DRESSING

This dressing is particularly good with greens and fruit. Try spring mix with pears and pecans or a green summer salad with peaches, blueberries, and almonds.

Ingredients

1/4 cup pure maple syrup
2 TBSP balsamic vinegar
1 tsp Dijon mustard

1/4 tsp salt
1/4 tsp pepper

Instructions

1   Mix all ingredients together (or shake in a jar). That's it!

MAKES: 1 CUP

SKILL LEVEL: 2 🥄🥄

TOTAL TIME: 10 MINUTES

GF

NF

For nut-free, replace the cashews and water with 3/4 cup silken tofu, non-dairy plain yogurt, or vegan mayonnaise.

MAKES: 6 TBSP

SKILL LEVEL: 1 🥄

TOTAL TIME: 5 MINUTES

GF

CILANTRO LIME
DRESSING

This is delicious on bean and rice burrito bowls or a green salad.

Ingredients

3/4 cup raw cashews

1/2 cup water

1 medium clove of garlic

Juice of 1 lime

A few dashes jalapeño tabasco sauce or spoonful of salsa verde

1/2 cup packed cilantro

1/2 tsp salt

Instructions

1 Blend cashews and water. Add the remaining ingredients and blend until smooth. Add a little more water to thin if necessary.

HONEY-LEMON
DRESSING

Ingredients

3 TBSP honey or maple syrup

3 TBSP fresh lemon juice (or lime)

Instructions

1 Stir together.

TIP

This dressing is delicious on a green salad with fruit (such as strawberries, apples, or mango), cooked quinoa, avocado, and glazed nuts.

142

CHIA JAM

You don't need a fancy recipe to make delicious jam! Chia seeds and berries are two of the most nutritious foods, and they go great together in this easy jam.

Ingredients

3 cups frozen berries
1/4 cup chia seeds

1/4 cup maple syrup or date paste

Instructions

1. Put the frozen berries in a large bowl. Let them thaw completely, either by microwaving them for about 3-5 minutes or by letting them sit on the counter for about 3 hours.

2. Mash the berries with a fork. Stir in the chia seeds and sweetener. Taste and add more sweetener until it's just right to you.

3. Let it sit in the fridge for at least 2 hours (preferably overnight). The chia seeds will be gelled and soft, not crunchy, and jam should be thick.

MAKES: 2 CUPS
SKILL LEVEL: 1
TOTAL TIME: 2+ HOURS

 GF NF

TIP
This jam lasts about 1 week in the fridge, or it can be frozen and then thawed later. It's delicious on pancakes, toast, cornbread, biscuits, or stirred into oatmeal.

A GUIDE TO POPCORN

Popcorn is a whole grain and can be a healthy snack if it's not covered in butter or too much salt. There are several ways to make popcorn. No matter the method, listen carefully for the sound of popping slowing down to know when it's done.

MICROWAVE

In a brown paper grocery bag or lunch bag, put 1/3 cup kernels. Fold the bag over a few times so the popcorn doesn't come out. Set microwave for 2 minutes 30 seconds, but you may need to stop the microwave when the pops slow down to about 3 seconds apart.

Instead of a paper bag, you can also put 1/2 cup kernels into a large glass bowl with a long paper towel or thin dish towel wrapped over it; or use a silicone microwave popcorn popper. Microwave for about 6 minutes, again listening for slowing popping to know if it's done early. Bowl will be hot!

STOVE TOP

Heat 2 TBSP oil in the bottom of a pot on medium heat. Put a couple popcorn kernels in and put a lid on it. When the tester kernels pop, add 1/2 cup kernels and put the lid back on quickly. Shake continuously until pops slow down to 2-3 seconds apart. Keep your face as far away from the pot as possible to avoid spurting oil.

AIR-POPPER

Put 1/2 cup kernels into the basket of the air popper. Plug it in and put a bowl in front to catch the popcorn. Unplug it when all the popcorn has popped.

TOPPINGS

To make the toppings stick, you'll need to first spray the popcorn with either water or oil. If you want to use water, get a small spray bottle or mister (use very little so the popcorn doesn't get soggy). For oil, use an oil-sprayer that will finely mist the popcorn. Have your seasoning ready to sprinkle on immediately so the water or oil is still wet and can make the seasonings stick.

For all these ideas, pop 1/2 cup kernels (about 10 cups popped popcorn). That's usually enough for 3-4 people.

CLASSIC

Spray with olive oil, then season with salt. Or, dilute 1 tsp salt in 1/2 cup water in a spray bottle and lightly spray the salty water onto the popcorn.

LIQUID AMINOS

You can buy Bragg Liquid Aminos in a small spray bottle, and it tastes great sprayed on popcorn. It has a salty taste but contains less sodium than straight salt. Don't use too much, or the popcorn will get soggy.

CHEESY

Spray the popcorn with water or oil and then sprinkle with nutritional yeast and salt.

KETTLE CORN

Preheat the oven to 350 degrees. Pour 1 TBSP maple syrup and 2 tsp of water into a small spray bottle. Spread the popcorn on a baking sheet. Spray the popcorn with the maple syrup mixture, then sprinkle with salt. Bake for 6-10 minutes until crispy. Let it cool.

PEANUT BUTTER CARAMEL CORN

Mix 1/4 cup peanut butter (or almond butter) and 1/4 cup maple syrup or honey together. Heat in the microwave for 30 seconds, until runny, then stir together. Pour over the popped popcorn and stir until coated. Try to not stir any unpopped kernels in, which could break a tooth!

Frozen Grapes

50+ WHOLE-FOOD SNACK IDEAS THAT DON'T REQUIRE A RECIPE

*M*ake a list of ideas that sound good to you and put it on your fridge!

- Celery with peanut butter and raisins
- Popcorn
- Frozen grapes
- Orange Mountains (orange slices sprinkled with shredded coconut and pulled into a line so triangle orange wedges look like mountain range with snow)
- Turtle Back Mango (cut mango on both sides of the pit, cut each slice into cubes, pop it out so it looks like turtle shell)
- Kiwi
- Any frozen fruit + frozen banana + plant milk blended up
- Baby carrots
- Cucumber slices
- Bell pepper strips
- Pumpkin seeds
- Sunflower seeds
- Dried figs
- Dried apricots
- Dried plums
- Banana with peanut butter
- Corn (either frozen, thawed, or on the cob)
- Berries (fresh or thawed from frozen)
- Frozen peas ("Peasicles!")
- Date with walnut or peanut butter inside
- Jicama sticks
- Baby tomatoes
- Pickles
- Olives
- Toast + applesauce + cinnamon

Turtle Back Mango

"Peasicles"

Monkey Toast

Orange Mountains

- Toast + avocado + smoked paprika, salt, and pepper
- Toast + hummus + tomato slices
- Almonds + raisins
- Pomegranate
- Grapefruit halves
- Pineapple chunks
- Papaya chunks
- Peach slices (fresh, canned, or thawed from frozen)
- Monkey toast: toast or rice cake + nut butter + apple or banana slices + chia seeds + honey
- Brazil nuts
- Cantaloupe
- Honeydew
- Baked sweet potato + salt and pepper
- Baked sweet potato + nut butter + berries + maple syrup
- Toasted corn tortillas + salsa + guacamole

- Brown rice + diced avocado + salt and pepper
- Tortilla + peanut butter + thinly sliced apple or banana, folded over
- Apple slices + peanut butter + hemp seeds
- Watermelon + frozen strawberries blended together
- Sugar snap peas
- Mini bell peppers
- Pistachios
- Edamame (thawed or cooked from frozen)
- Seaweed
- Chopped apple + lemon juice + drizzled maple syrup + chopped nuts + cinnamon
- Cookie Dough Dip: mix equal parts peanut butter and plant milk, then stir in a blip of maple syrup and some mini chocolate chips and serve with apple slices

WHAT IS NUTRIENT DENSITY?

*n*utrients are tiny compounds in food that help our bodies work properly and stay healthy. Some foods have lots of nutrients, while others don't.

Think of nutrients like value and calories like money. You don't want to use up all your money on something that isn't valuable! And we don't want to eat lots of calories and not get the nutrients our bodies need. Nutrient density is how much nutrition we get for the calories consumed, like how much value we get for the money spent. Eating 200 calories and getting almost no nutrients is like spending $200 and only getting a pencil. What a rip-off!

1 CUP GRAPES	VS	1 SMALL CHOCOLATE CHIP COOKIE
62 calories		120 calories
0 g fat		5 g fat
1 g fiber		0 g fiber
1 g protein		1 g protein
Vitamins C, A, and antioxidants		No vitamins
1 ingredient (a whole food)		15 or more ingredients (a processed food)

1 CUP BLUEBERRIES	VS	1 POUCH FRUIT SNACKS
85 calories		80 calories
0.5 g fat		0 g fat
3.6 g fiber		0 g fiber
24% natural vitamin C		25% added vitamin C
Tons of antioxidants		Little to no antioxidants
1 ingredient (a whole food)		19 ingredients (a processed food)

Foods without many nutrients are referred to as being full of "empty calories." They still give us energy, but not any superpower nutrients. They may even rob our bodies of the nutrients they already have. We might choose to eat less nutritious foods as part of a celebration or special circumstance, but to have good health, we should eat mostly whole plant foods, which have lots of value!

These charts illustrate how similar amounts of food vary widely in nutrient density. Nutrition, energy, and enjoyment affect the value of each food to us.

2 CUPS ROMAINE LETTUCE	1 TABLESPOON CANOLA OIL
20 calories	120 calories
0 g fat	14 g fat
1 g fiber	0 g fiber
0 g protein	0 g protein
Tons of antioxidants and micronutrients	No micronutrients, no antioxidants

1/2 CUP COOKED BLACK BEANS	1/2 CUP CHOCOLATE CHIPS
114 calories	402 calories
0.4 g fat	25 g fat
7.6 g protein	3.3 g protein
7.5 g fiber	5 g fiber
1 ingredient (a whole food)	6 ingredients (a processed food)

1/2 CUP CORN (3 OUNCES)	1 OUNCE CORN TORTILLA CHIPS
60 calories	140 calories
0.4 g fat	7 g fat
2 g protein	2 g protein
2 g fiber	2 g fiber
1 ingredient (a whole food)	3 or more ingredients (a processed food)

DESSERT

DID YOU KNOW?

In a study of cyclists and triathlon athletes, raisins worked just as well as sports jelly beans to improve performance and replenish glycogen stores. No need to buy special or expensive energy gels for your next long-distance race—raisins are just as effective![23]

OATMEAL RAISIN
BEE BITES

MAKES: 15-20 BEES
SKILL LEVEL: 2
TOTAL TIME: 30 MINUTES
GF

Oatmeal raisin cookies in bee form, buzzing right toward you!

Ingredients

1/2 cup raisins

1/2 cup chopped dates (or 1/4 cup maple syrup)

1/4 cup almond butter (or any nut/seed butter)

1/2 tsp cinnamon

1 tsp vanilla extract

1 cup rolled oats

1/8 tsp salt

1/4 cup chocolate chips (optional)

FOR DECORATION

Slivered almonds

Toothpicks

Cocoa powder or 2 TBSP melted chocolate chips

Instructions

1 Soak the raisins and dates in hot water for about 10 minutes. Drain.

2 Put the raisins and dates in a food processor and process until the raisins and dates are well-chopped and they start to form a ball.

3 Add the remaining ingredients and process until well-combined. If the dough is too sticky, let it sit for 20 minutes for the oats to absorb moisture, or blend in a tablespoon or two of extra oats.

4 Form dough into small, oval bee bodies. Dip a toothpick in cocoa powder or melted chocolate and draw stripes across the back of each. Use a clean toothpick to poke two eyes and a smile in front. Poke two slivered almonds in for wings.

5 Eat right away, or store the bees in the fridge for up to one week.

Medjool Dates

Deglet Noor Dates

A NOTE ABOUT DATES

The two types of dates most commonly found in grocery stores are Medjool and Deglet Noor. Medjool dates are large and very sweet and caramel-like, but are more expensive. Deglet Noor dates are smaller and more dry, and are also cheaper. All varieties of dates provide sweetness with lots of fiber and are good choices for healthy treats.

APPLE NACHOS

Ingredients

CARAMEL SAUCE

6-8 large Medjool dates (or 12 Deglet Noor dates—see opposite note)

1/2 cup light coconut milk (or any plant milk)

1/4 cup water

1 tsp vanilla extract

APPLE NACHOS

4 apples (2-4 different varieties and colors is nice)

1/4 cup peanut butter or almond butter

Shredded coconut

Chopped nuts

Hemp seeds

Dried cranberries

Mini chocolate chips

Instructions

1. Blend all the caramel sauce ingredients together in a small blender until very smooth. If your dates are hard, you may need to let the sauce ingredients soak together for about 10 minutes, and then blend again to get it really smooth.

2. Cut apples into thin slices. Arrange apple slices on a plate. Slightly melt nut butter in the microwave for 30 seconds if it's stiff.

3. Drizzle caramel sauce and then peanut or almond butter over the apples. Sprinkle with coconut, chopped nuts, hemp seeds, dried cranberries, and chocolate chips as you desire.

NUTRITIONAL BENEFITS
Apples contain a soluble fiber called pectin that has many health benefits. It helps good bacteria flourish in your gut, may relieve both diarrhea and constipation, helps your liver remove toxins and heavy metals from your body, and the pectin even improves cholesterol levels and blood pressure. Better make these super-tasty apple nachos a regular thing! [24, 25]

More Popsicle Recipes

BANANA CHOCOLATE PEANUT BUTTER POPSICLES

1/2 cup plant milk

2 large, ripe bananas (fresh or frozen)

1/4 cup peanut butter (or peanut butter powder for lower fat)

2 TBSP cocoa powder

1 tsp vanilla

1 TBSP maple syrup or 2 dates (if needed for sweetness)

1. Blend together and taste for sweetness. Pour into molds and freeze. Makes 4–6, depending on size.

PIÑA COLADA POPSICLES

1/2 cup light coconut milk or soy milk

1 cup frozen mango

2 cups frozen pineapple

1 cup fresh or frozen banana chunks

1 TBSP maple syrup (optional)

1. Blend together and pour into molds and freeze.

RASPBERRY LEMONADE POPSICLES

1 can light coconut milk or 1 1/2 cups soy milk

3 cups frozen pineapple

1/4 cup maple syrup

1/4 cup fresh lemon juice

2 tsp lemon zest

1. Blend together, then stir in 1 cup frozen raspberries. Pour into molds and freeze.

COCONUT LIME
POPSICLES

MAKES: 6-10 POPSICLES, DEPENDING ON SIZE
SKILL LEVEL: 2
TOTAL TIME: 4 HOURS

GF **NF**

Ingredients

2-3 limes
1 can (14 oz) light coconut milk
3 cups (10 oz) frozen pineapple

1 cup packed fresh spinach
1/4 cup maple syrup

Instructions

1. Wash the limes well. Zest them with a fine grater or zester. Collect at least 1 tsp lime zest.

2. Cut and juice the limes to get at least 4 TBSP lime juice.

3. Blend all the ingredients in a blender until completely smooth. Taste and add more lime juice or maple syrup until it's perfectly sweet and lime-y.

4. Pour into popsicle molds and freeze for at least 4 hours. Run hot water over the mold to help them slip out easily.

TIP
You can use soy milk instead of coconut milk for lower fat. Popsicles will be more icy, but still yummy!

TIP

Instead of strawberries, you could use canned mandarin oranges like worms or decorate with some fresh flowers (just don't eat them!).

Our Strawberry Patch

DIRT CUPS

These are not only very fun and cute, but one of the most decadent and delicious desserts you could make! This dessert is high in protein, calcium, iron, magnesium, and vitamin E. It is also very high in fat, so make it just for special occasions.

MAKES: 4 LARGE CUPS
SKILL LEVEL: 2
PREP TIME: 15 MINUTES (PLUS 1 HOUR CHILLING TIME)

GF NF (without peanut butter)

Ingredients

PUDDING
3/4 cup non-dairy chocolate chips
1 package firm silken tofu (must be silken)
1/4 cup peanut butter (optional)
1 tsp vanilla

DIRT
1/2 cup dates
1/2 cup almonds (or any nut or seed)
2 TBSP ground flax seeds
1 TBSP cocoa powder
1/4 tsp salt
1/2 tsp vanilla

DECORATION
Strawberries and cups for serving

Instructions

1. Melt the chocolate chips in a bowl in the microwave for 1-2 minutes until smooth when stirred.

2. Empty the package of silken tofu into a blender. Add the melted chocolate chips, peanut butter (if using), and vanilla. Blend until smooth.

3. Divide the pudding into cups or little jars and put in the fridge for at least 1 hour to set up. While it chills, make the dirt.

4. In a food processor, blend the dates until sticky. Add the almonds, flax seeds, cocoa, salt, and vanilla and process until crumbly.

5. Sprinkle the dirt onto the pudding. Add a strawberry on top and enjoy eating dirt!

PUMPKIN ORANGES

Speaking of pumpkins, a fun fall-time game is to draw faces on tangerines or clementines so they look like pumpkins. Then, hide them in your yard and go for a pumpkin hunt! They are colorful, sweet, and pre-wrapped, just like candy!

PUMPKIN
CHOCOLATE CHIP
COOKIES

MAKES: 15 COOKIES
SKILL LEVEL: 2
TOTAL TIME: 50 MINUTES

 GF NF

Ingredients

DRY INGREDIENTS
1 1/4 cup oat flour (blend 1 1/4 cup oats in blender until fine)
1 tsp baking powder
1/4 tsp salt
2 tsp Pumpkin Spice Blend (see page 126)

WET INGREDIENTS
3/4 cup pumpkin purée
2 tsp vanilla extract
1/2 cup pure maple syrup

MIX-INS
1/2 cup chocolate chips

Instructions

1 Mix dry ingredients together.

2 In a large liquid measuring cup, mix pumpkin, vanilla, and maple syrup together. Stir into dry ingredients. Then, stir in chocolate chips.

3 Let the dough chill in the fridge for at least 10 minutes so the oats can absorb some of the moisture. Meanwhile, heat the oven to 325 degrees.

4 Spoon heaping-tablespoon-size cookies onto a parchment-lined baking sheet. Get your fingers wet and press each cookie to flatten it a bit.

5 Bake for 15-17 minutes. Let cool on the baking sheet for at least 10 minutes to allow them to set before moving (or eating!).

HOT COCOA

Make yourself a steaming cup of healthy hot cocoa!

MAKES: 1 SERVING
SKILL LEVEL: 1
TOTAL TIME: 5 MINUTES

GF NF

Ingredients

1 cup plant milk

2 tsp cacao powder

1-2 TBSP maple syrup, honey, or date paste (choose how sweet you want it)

1/8 tsp salt

EXTRA FLAVOR (OPTIONAL)

1/2 tsp vanilla extract

A pinch of ground ginger

1 drop peppermint essential oil

1/4 tsp Pumpkin Spice Blend (see page 126)

Instructions

1 Mix all ingredients in a microwave-safe mug or small saucepan.

2 Microwave mug for 1 minute, or warm in saucepan on the stove for about 5 minutes on medium heat. Test temperature with your finger before drinking and add some cold milk if necessary to cool it down.

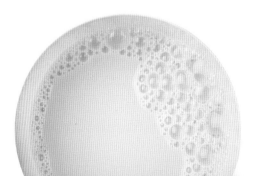

Healthy Chocolate Frosting

INGREDIENTS

1 orange sweet
potato (yam)

1/4 cup unsweetened
cocoa powder

1 cup dates, soaked
in hot water at
least 10 minutes

1/4 cup nut butter
(such as peanut
butter or almond
butter)

1 tsp vanilla extract
(optional)

1/4 tsp salt

1/4 cup plant milk

1/2 cup chocolate
chips, melted (can
be omitted for
lower sugar)

INSTRUCTIONS

1. Cook sweet potato by microwaving it
   for about 8 minutes or by baking it in a
   425-degree oven for about 40 minutes.
   Once cool, scoop out 1 cup of mashed baked
   potato.

2. If you'd like to add chocolate chips, melt
   them for 60 seconds in the microwave. Put
   all ingredients into a bullet or high-
   speed blender. Blend, stir, and blend again
   until smooth, adding an extra 1/4 cup milk
   if necessary to help it blend.

3. Taste and add maple syrup or other
   sweetener of choice if desired. If you'd
   like a darker chocolate flavor, add up to
   1/4 cup more cocoa powder.

The dates thicken it up with time. Store in
the fridge for up to 1 week. It can be piped as
cake decorating frosting, eaten with fruit,
or spread on rice cakes or pancakes.

Makes 2 cups. For nut-free, omit the nut
butter completely.

ZECRETLY HEALTHY
CHOCOLATE
CUPCAKES

MAKES: 12 LARGE MUFFINS
SKILL LEVEL: 2
TOTAL TIME: 40 MINUTES

For gluten-free, use 1 3/4 cups certified gluten-free oat flour instead of 1 1/4 cups whole wheat flour.

Ingredients

DRY INGREDIENTS
1 1/4 cups whole wheat flour
1 tsp baking soda
1/4 tsp salt
1/3 cup cocoa powder

WET INGREDIENTS
1 flax "egg" (1 TBSP ground flax seeds mixed with 3 TBSP water)

1 ripe mashed banana (about 3/4 cup)
1/3 cup maple syrup
1 TBSP vinegar
1 tsp vanilla extract
1 cup grated zucchini
1 cup grated carrot

MIX-INS
1/2 cup chocolate chips

Instructions

1. Preheat the oven to 350 degrees. Get out a silicone muffin pan or grease a regular muffin pan.

2. In a small bowl, mix the ground flax seeds with the water to create an egg substitute.

3. In a mixing bowl, mix the dry ingredients together.

4. In another large bowl, mash the bananas. Stir in the maple syrup, vinegar, vanilla, flax "egg," zucchini, and carrot.

5. Mix in the dry ingredients, then stir in the chocolate chips.

6. Scoop the batter into muffin cups. Bake mini muffins for 12-15 minutes and bake regular muffins for 20-23 minutes, or until they bounce back when touched.

7. Let cool completely before eating. Eat by themselves or with chocolate frosting and a glass of ice-cold plant milk.

TIP
These cupcakes last in the fridge for 5 days, and freeze very well for up to 3 months.

A NOTE ABOUT USING FRESH FRUIT

Fruits taste best and are most affordable when they are in season. When they're not, frozen or canned work well for desserts like this, too. Here are fruits that are in season during each part of the year.

SPRING

Cherries	Strawberries
Apricots	

SUMMER

Blackberries	Plums
Blueberries	Raspberries
Nectarines	Melons
Peaches	

FALL

Apples	Grapes
Pears	Pears
Cranberries	Pomegranates
Figs	

WINTER

Oranges	Grapefruits

FRUIT COBBLER

Ingredients

FILLING

4 cups thinly sliced peaches, berries, or cherries (either fresh, frozen, or canned)

1/4 cup maple syrup (if you think the fruit is not sweet enough)

1 TBSP cornstarch

1 tsp vanilla

1/4 tsp salt

COBBLER TOPPING

3/4 cup whole wheat flour

3/4 cup almond flour

1 1/2 tsp baking powder

1/4 tsp salt

2/3 cup plant milk

1/3 cup maple syrup

Instructions

1. Preheat oven to 375 degrees.

2. Get out a 9x13-inch pan (slightly smaller also works).

3. If using frozen fruit, thaw it out first (in the microwave or let it sit for several hours). If using canned, drain it well.

4. Mix the fruit, maple syrup, cornstarch, vanilla, and salt together in the baking pan.

5. In a bowl, stir the cobbler topping ingredients together. Spoon the batter over the fruit into several blobs, then spread it together to cover the fruit.

6. Bake for 30-35 minutes, or until topping is firm to the touch.

7. Let it cool slightly before serving. Serve alone, or with a dollop of non-dairy yogurt or Nice Cream (see page 170).

NF For nut-free, omit the almond flour and increase the baking flour by 3/4 cup. Use full-fat coconut milk as the plant milk for the best texture, since there will be no fat from the almond flour.

GF For gluten-free, use 1/2 cup certified gluten-free oat flour and 1/4 cup all-purpose gluten-free flour in place of whole wheat flour.

CHOCOLATE CHIP {CHICKPEA} COOKIE BARS

This is one of our all-time favorite desserts. Don't tell anyone about the chickpeas until *after* they taste it!

Ingredients

1 (15 oz) can chickpeas or white beans, drained
1/3 cup maple syrup OR 1 cup soft dates
1/2 cup peanut butter or almond butter
1/2 cup oat flour
2 TBSP ground flax seeds

1/4 tsp baking soda
1/2 tsp baking powder
1/4 tsp salt
1 tsp vanilla extract
3/4 cup semi-sweet or dark chocolate chips

Instructions

1. Preheat oven to 350 degrees. Line an 8x8-inch square pan with parchment paper or grease it.

2. Process the first three ingredients in a food processor or high-speed blender, scraping down the sides often so the chickpeas get well-blended. If using dates, add 2 TBSP water.

3. Add the remaining ingredients (except chocolate chips) and process until smooth.

4. Stir in the chocolate chips. Taste the dough and add additional maple syrup if desired. Spread the batter into the pan and sprinkle a few more chocolate chips on top.

5. Bake for 35-40 minutes until golden on the edges and a toothpick comes out mostly clean.

6. Let cool completely before cutting into bars with a plastic knife (plastic cuts bars cleaner). Sprinkle lightly with sea salt for an extra touch. Remove with a spatula. Enjoy with a glass of plant milk or Nice Cream on top!

MAKES: 9 LARGE BARS
SKILL LEVEL: 2
TOTAL TIME: 45 MINUTES

For nut-free, replace peanut butter with tahini or sunflower butter.

TIP

You can use brown sugar or coconut sugar instead of maple syrup, but omit the oat flour, since the dough will be more dry.

TIP

To bake these into cookies instead of bars, scoop 20-25 small balls of dough onto a baking sheet and press down with your fingers to flatten them slightly. Bake for 20 minutes and then let cool completely.

Variations

For each variation, add its ingredients to 2 cups of frozen bananas and blend until smooth.

CHOCOLATE: 1 TBSP cocoa powder + 1 tsp vanilla + pinch of salt

PEANUT BUTTER CUP: 1 TBSP cocoa powder + 2 TBSP peanut butter + chocolate chips

CHERRY: 1 cup frozen cherries + 1 tsp vanilla or 1/2 tsp almond extract

MINT CHIP: Handful of spinach + chocolate chips + 1 drop peppermint extract

PIÑA COLADA: 1 cup frozen pineapple + 1/4 cup coconut flakes

PEANUT BUTTER: 2 TBSP peanut butter

SALTED CARAMEL: 4 large dates + pinch of salt

STRAWBERRY: 1 cup frozen strawberries

LEMON BERRY: 1 cup mixed berries + squeeze of lemon juice

PUMPKIN PIE: 1/4 cup pumpkin purée + 1 tsp pumpkin pie spice + 1-2 TBSP maple syrup

PEACHES 'N' CREAM: 2 cups frozen peaches + 1 tsp vanilla

A GUIDE TO NICE CREAM

*N*ice Cream is like ice cream, but made from frozen bananas that are blended up like soft-serve! It's creamy, sweet, and delicious. This recipe will make enough for two large servings.

HOW TO MAKE NICE CREAM

Ingredients

2 ripe bananas (just a few brown spots is perfect)

Instructions

FREEZING THE BANANAS (THIS CAN BE DONE AHEAD OF TIME)

1. Peel the bananas, cut them into slices, and put them in a zip-top bag.

2. Set the bag in the freezer flat, with space between the bananas, so they don't all freeze in one big clump.

3. Once frozen (usually in just a few hours), proceed to make the Nice Cream. Or, save for a later time!

MAKING THE NICE CREAM

1. Put some frozen bananas in a high-speed blender (a food processor also works) and let them sit for 5-10 minutes to slightly thaw.

2. Blend until smooth, stopping frequently to stir if necessary. Add a small splash of plant milk if necessary to get your blender going.

3. Add a small amount of maple syrup, or blend in soft dates if you want it sweeter. Add some cashews or cashew butter if you'd like it creamier. Blend until very smooth.

Here are two of our favorite Nice Cream recipes that don't need bananas!

CHOCOLATE CHERRY NICE CREAM

This is my daughter Charity's favorite treat, so we call it Chocolate Cherr-ity Ice Cream.

4 large, soft dates
1/3 cup plant milk
1 TBSP cacao powder

1/2 tsp almond or vanilla extract (optional)
2 cups frozen cherries (10 oz)

1. Blend the dates, milk, cacao, and extract together first. Then add cherries and blend until smooth, adding a splash of extra milk if necessary to help it blend.

PINEAPPLE DOLE WHIP

2 cups frozen pineapple chunks
1/4 cup canned coconut milk

1 cup frozen mango chunks or frozen banana (optional)

1. In a food processor, process the pineapple (and other fruit, if using) until it's chopped into fine pieces (you can use a blender, but it won't "whip" up quite the same).

2. Add the coconut milk and run the food processor for at least a full minute until very smooth and light and fluffy. Enjoy immediately for best texture, or store in the freezer. Add a sweetener of choice if you feel necessary, but we think it's delicious on its own.

WHY WHOLE FOODS ARE BEST

A lot of plant foods sold in stores are processed, meaning the foods have parts taken away or have other ingredients added to them. Some processing is often necessary to preserve or transport food (such as canned fruits or vegetables). However, when foods are overly processed, they become much less valuable to our bodies. They can also become addictive.

Here are some easy ways to tell the difference between a whole food and a processed food:

- Whole foods have one ingredient. Processed foods have lots of ingredients.
- Whole foods come straight from a tree or plant. Processed foods come from factories.
- Whole foods have all their nutrition. Processed foods have some or all nutrition taken away.

Most whole foods do not have ingredient labels, like apples and bananas in the store. However, when buying packaged foods, look for ones that have 1–3 ingredients. For example, the best peanut butter is made of just peanuts. The best rice cakes are made of just brown rice.

Some foods are made of lots of whole foods, and those can be good choices. For example, salsa is made of tomatoes, onions, peppers, and spices, which are whole foods combined together. True corn tortillas are made of just corn and water.

Some examples of processed foods that don't have much nutrition are oil, white flour, and white sugar. These foods have had all the healthy parts taken away, so they are empty calories (they give us energy but not nutrients—see page 148 for more about nutrient density). To feel our best, we should limit how often we buy foods with these ingredients in them. These foods are not only empty calories, but they can also rob us of nutrition we already have in our bodies.

Not everything we eat has to be a whole food, but the more whole foods we eat, the healthier we'll be and the better we'll feel!

ACTIVITY SHEET Help your kids find more healthy options with our fun activity sheet! Download for free at faithfulplateful.com/printable-worksheets (or simply scan the QR code).

ASK YOUR CHILD: **CAN YOU TELL WHICH OF THESE FOODS ARE WHOLE AND WHICH OF THESE FOODS ARE PROCESSED? (SOME MIGHT NOT BE OBVIOUS—DISCUSS WHY!)**

173

SAMPLE MENUS

SUMMER PARTY

- Confetti Black Bean Salsa with Toaster Chips (73)
- Watermelon
- Pineapple Dole Whip (171)
- Coconut Lime Popsicles (157)
- Three-Ingredient Sweet Potato BBQ Sandwiches (65)
- Bravo Bean Burgers (83)
- Sushi Rolls (70)
- Nice Cream Bar or Smoothie Bowl Bar (let everyone put their own toppings on) (170 + 44)
- Fruit Kabobs
- Bread Bunny Veggie Tray with Ranch Dip (129 + 137)

WINTER PARTY

- Veggies with Yummest Hummus (115)
- Mouse Baked Potatoes (87)
- Curried Rice with Veggies (67)
- Alphabet Soup with Breadsticks (91)
- Apple Nachos (155)
- Pumpkin Chocolate Chip Cookies (161)
- Hot Cocoa (163)

MEXICAN FIESTA

- Build-Your-Own Burrito Bowls or Nachos
- Confetti Black Bean Salsa with Toaster Chips (73)
- Taquitos (99)
- Lentil Tacos (97)
- The Three Bears' Overnight Porridge (use rice for arroz con leche-type dessert) (43)
- Bean "Quesadillas" (63)

MOTHER'S DAY OR FATHER'S DAY BREAKFAST

- Breakfast Burritos (31)
- Smashed Potatoes (47)
- Smoothies (44)
- Banana Mini Muffins (131)
- Fruit Salad
- Pancakes with Homemade Nutella and Fruit (33 + 40)
- Nice Cream (makes a special breakfast!) (170)
- Breakfast Charcuterie Board (133)

BRUNCH

- Build-Your-Own Oatmeal Bar (48 + 50)
- Pancake Bar (33)
- Smoothies (44)
- Mini Chia Pudding Cups (37)
- Fruit Salad
- Veggies and Ranch Dip (137)
- Smashed Potatoes (47)

MAKE-AHEAD PICNIC

- Chickpea Salad Sandwiches (57)
- Peanut Butter and Banana Sandwiches
- Pasta Salad (69)
- Bean and Rice Burritos
- Confetti Black Bean Salsa with Toaster Chips (73)
- Raw Veggies
- Fruit
- Energy Balls (123)
- Banana Mini Muffins (131)
- Fruit leather or dried fruit

About the Author

FAITH RALPHS lives in Idaho with her husband and children. She has a degree in Public Health from Brigham Young University. Faith has been employed as a health coach for five years and is the face behind FaithfulPlateful.com. Since she was a young girl, she has loved making food for others and learning about nutrition. When not making a mess in the kitchen or cleaning it up, she likes to run, hike, travel, and do anything outside in nature. Some of her current favorite foods are pancakes loaded with fresh strawberries and bananas on top, chickpea salad sandwiches on homemade sourdough bread, white bean chili, and chocolate cherry Nice Cream.

For more recipes, check out FaithfulPlateful.com and follow on Instagram and Facebook @faithful.plateful.

If you liked this book, please leave a review online at your favorite retailer. Honest reviews spread the word about Bushel & Peck—and help us make better books, too!

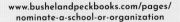

www.bushelandpeckbooks.com/pages/nominate-a-school-or-organization

Endnotes

1. "Selected Health Conditions and Risk Factors, by Age: United States, Selected Years 1988-1994 through 2017-2018." Centers for Disease Control and Prevention, March 2, 2021. https://www.cdc.gov/nchs/hus/contents2019.htm#Table-021.

2. "1 in 5 Adolescents and 1 in 4 Young Adults Now Living with Prediabetes." Centers for Disease Control and Prevention, December 2, 2019. https://www.cdc.gov/media/releases/2019/p1202-diabetes.html.

3. GMFH Editing Team. "Does a Plant-Based Diet Improve Gut Health? An Interview with Hana Kahleova." Gut Microbiota for Health, June 17, 2020. https://www.gutmicrobiotaforhealth.com/does-a-plant-based-diet-improve-gut-health-an-interview-with-hana-kahleova/.

4. Greger, Michael. "Childhood Constipation and Cow's Milk." NutritionFacts.org, August 18, 2014. https://nutritionfacts.org/video/childhood-constipation-and-cows-milk/.

5. Fuhrman, Joel. *Disease-Proof Your Child: Feeding Kids Right.* New York: St. Martin's Griffin, 2006.

6. Alwarith, Jihad, Hana Kahleova, Lee Crosby, Alexa Brooks, Lizoralia Brandon, Susan M Levin, and Neal D Barnard. "The Role of Nutrition in Asthma Prevention and Treatment." Nutrition reviews. Oxford University Press, November 1, 2020. https://www.ncbi.nlm.nih.gov/pmc/articles/PMC7550896/.

7. "Plant-Based Diets." Physicians Committee for Responsible Medicine, n.d. https://www.pcrm.org/good-nutrition/plant-based-diets.

8. Lucas, Tamara, and Richard Horton. "Food in the Anthropocene: The Eat- Lancet Commission on Healthy Diets" The Lancet, n.d. https://www.thelancet.com/commissions/EAT.

9. "The 900 Gallon Diet: Meat, Portion Size and Water Footprints." Water Footprint Calculator, May 24, 2022. https://www.watercalculator.org/footprint/meat-portions-900-gallons/.

10. Environmental Working Group. "Dirty Dozen™ Fruits and Vegetables with the Most Pesticides." EWG's 2022 Shopper's Guide to Pesticides in Produce, Dirty Dozen, n.d. https://www.ewg.org/foodnews/dirty-dozen.php.

11. "Nutrition Comparison: Tofu vs Milk." Soupersage, n.d. https://www.soupersage.com/compare-nutrition/tofu-vs-milk.

12. "Flaxseeds." NutritionFacts.org, n.d. https://nutritionfacts.org/topics/flax-seeds/.

13. Shukla, Alpana P., Radu G. Iliescu, Catherine E. Thomas, and Louis J. Aronne. "Food Order Has a Significant Impact on Postprandial Glucose and Insulin Levels." American Diabetes Association, June 11, 2015. https://diabetesjournals.org/care/article/38/7/e98/30914/Food-Order-Has-a-Significant-Impact-on.

14. Coyle, Daisy. "9 Impressive Health Benefits of Beets." Healthline. Healthline Media, November 11, 2021. https://www.healthline.com/nutrition/benefits-of-beets.

15. Buettner, Dan. *The Blue Zones Solution: Eating and Living like the World's Healthiest People.* Washington, DC: National Geographic, 2017.

16. Piazza, Geri. "How Too Little Potassium May Contribute to Cardiovascular Disease." National Institutes of Health. U.S. Department of Health and Human Services, October 31, 2017. https://www.nih.gov/news-events/nih-research-matters/how-too-little-potassium-may-contribute-cardiovascular-disease.

17. Greger, Michael. "Is Milk Good for Our Bones?" NutritionFacts.org, March 16, 2015. https://nutritionfacts.org/video/is-milk-good-for-our-bones/.

18. Nicastro, Holly L., Sharon A. Ross, and John A. Milner. "Garlic and Onions: Their Cancer Prevention Properties." Cancer prevention research (Philadelphia, Pa.). U.S. National Library of Medicine, March 2015. https://www.ncbi.nlm.nih.gov/pmc/articles/PMC4366009/.

19. Boehrer, Katherine. "Which of Your Favorite Foods Are Hiding a Massive Water Footprint?" HuffPost. December 31, 2018. https://www.huffpost.com/entry/food-water-footprint_n_5952862.

20. Greger, Michael, and Gene Stone. *How Not to Die.* New York: Flatiron Books, 2015.

21. Waghorn, Mark. "Popeye Was Right: Spinach Really Does Make Your Muscles Stronger." Study Finds, March 24, 2021. https://www.studyfinds.org/spinach-make-muscles-stronger/.

22. Fuhrman, Joel. "The Cancer-Fighting Power of Cruciferous Vegetables." Dr. Fuhrman, n.d. https://www.drfuhrman.com/blog/209/the-cancer-fighting-power-of-cruciferous-vegetables.

23. Rietschier, Helena L., Tara M. Henagan, Conrad P. Earnest, Birgitta L. Baker, Cory C. Cortez, and Laura K. Stewart. "Sun-Dried Raisins Are a Cost-Effective Alternative to Sports Jelly Beans in Prolonged Cycling." *Journal of Strength and Conditioning Research.* U.S. National Library of Medicine, n.d. https://pubmed.ncbi.nlm.nih.gov/21881533/.

24. Wartenberg, Lisa. "10 Promising Benefits and Uses of Apple Pectin." Healthline. Healthline Media, June 14, 2021. https://www.healthline.com/nutrition/apple-pectin#4.-May-aid-heart-health https://www.thistle.co/learn/thistle-thoughts/detoxification-detox-foods-for-health.

25. Lowe, Ashley. "Detoxification: Detox Foods for a Healthier You." Thistle, n.d. https://www.thistle.co/learn/thistle-thoughts/detoxification-detox-foods-for-health.